The Zoning of America

LANDMARK LAW CASES

AMERICAN SOCIETY

Peter Charles Hoffer
N. E. H. Hull
Series Editors

MICHAEL ALLAN WOLF

The Zoning of America

Euclid v. Ambler

UNIVERSITY PRESS OF KANSAS

Published by the University Press of Kansas (Lawrence, Kansas 66045), which was organized by the Kansas Board of Regents and is operated and funded by Emporia State University, Fort Hays State University, Kansas State University, Pittsburg State University, the University of Kansas, and Wichita State University

Library of Congress Cataloging-in-Publication Data

Wolf, Michael Allan.

The zoning of America : Euclid v. Ambler / Michael Allan Wolf.

p. cm.—(Landmark law cases & American society)

Includes bibliographical references and index.

ISBN 978-0-7006-1620-6 (cloth : alk. paper)

ISBN 978-0-7006-1621-3 (pbk. : alk. paper)

1. Zoning law—United States. 2. Zoning law—United States—Cases. I. Title.

KF5692.W65 2008

346.7304'5—dc22

2008012308

British Library Cataloguing-in-Publication Data is available.

Printed in the United States of America

10 9 8 7 6 5 4 3 2

The paper used in this publication is recycled and contains 50 percent postconsumer waste. It is acid free and meets the minimum requirements of the American National Standard for Permanence of Paper for Printed Library Materials Z39.48-1992.

For my parents:

Leonard Wolf (of blessed memory) and Rhoda Bernard Wolf

CONTENTS

Village of Euclid v. Ambler Realty Co. (1926) was a hard case, in many ways a novel case, and one whose origins and course had fallen into obscurity. Michael Allan Wolf's superb detective work in archives, newspapers, and court records brings to light a remarkable story, not only of the case that made zoning a feature of nearly every city and town in America, but of the American landscape itself. Involving one of the most respected lawyers of the 1920s, calling forth friends of the court briefs from experts, special interests, and urban planners, the case deserves its place in a series of landmark litigations.

The issue was whether a Cleveland, Ohio, suburb could ordain land use, determining which zones would be residential, which commercial, and which industrial; how high buildings might be; and whether certain industries could locate themselves within the village limits. The village council meetings were models of local democracy, though the ordinance immediately met opposition from Ambler Realty, speaking for itself and other developers. Could a town or city deny to property owners the rights to use their land? Nuisance abatement had long been a feature of American land law, but a comprehensive scheme of regulation, that was something else.

Or was it? Wolf locates the case not only in the law, but in the history of urban development. Cleveland was not only the first real city in the Western Reserve, its development recapitulated the urbanization of America. From farming mart to commercial center to industrial giant, Cleveland's was a success story. But reformers in the early twentieth century, led by progressive city planners, advocates of beautification, landscape architects, mass transportation entrepreneurs, and chambers of commerce, had designs for what would have been unregulated sprawl. Euclid stood at the "crossroads" of these stories, and in 1922 it joined a number of other cities and towns in balancing residential and business land use.

As all politics is local; so is all land-use planning, but the assault on the Euclid ordinance, and the defense of it, burst onto the national stage. When the case arrived at the U.S. Supreme Court, savvy odds-makers would have given Euclid little chance — but chance, in the form of a dogged city planner, a personally committed attorney, a new member of the High Court, and a mysterious about-face, threw the odds out the window.

Wolf's meticulous presentation of the legal issues, his reconstruction of the dramatic course of litigation in which no victory was safe and no defeat final, his lively biographical vignettes taking the reader inside the Taft Court, make a legal story into a compelling human drama. Land law, sometimes the driest of all subjects, in Wolf's hands comes alive. This is a model essay, and must reading for students of city planning, land-use law, the Taft Court, and Progressive Era America.

The reader will learn in the pages that follow that the story of *Euclid v. Ambler* is intimately tied to the history of metropolitan Cleveland, Ohio. The house in which I lived from birth until the day I left home for college is located one block from Cleveland Heights Boulevard, my first public school is named Cleveland Court Elementary, and I learned to play golf at the Cleveland Heights Golf Course. Yet it was not until I was in my fifties that I first set foot in Cleveland, Ohio, or, for that matter, in any of its suburbs, including Cleveland Heights. A Cleveland area real estate developer named H. A. Stahl is the missing link that ties my first neighborhood – located in Lakeland, Florida, in the heart of the Sunshine State – to the Buckeye State's largest city.

Seeking to capitalize on the fact that the Cleveland Indians had selected Lakeland for its spring training home in the early 1920s, the city's Chamber of Commerce encouraged Stahl to ply his trade in central Florida. In 1924, Stahl responded to the entreaties by acquiring 560 acres on the south side of picturesque Lake Hollingsworth for more than $900,000. The name Stahl chose for his development – Cleveland Heights – was, therefore, not surprising. Nor is the fact that many of the streets that he laid out in the neighborhood still carry the same names as those found in that older suburb of Cleveland. The golf course opened one year later, but in 1927, after hard times hit the Florida real estate market, the ambitious developer was forced to sell the course and clubhouse to the city. Other developers and builders would pick up where Stahl left off, maintaining the residential character of the Cleveland Heights section of Lakeland by private controls (particularly restrictive covenants that controlled the kinds of activities permitted on the land and, in many instances, the race and religion of potential owners) and by public regulations (chiefly zoning).

The 1920s were a crucial decade in the history of American zoning in communities in Florida and Ohio, indeed in most parts of the country that were experiencing a sharp growth in residential developments located miles from a traditional city center. The U.S. Supreme Court would not definitively determine the constitutional soundness of zoning – a relatively new, though popular, tool for regulating the use of land – until November of 1926, by which time millions of Americans were living in "zoned" cities and towns in every region of the country. With the Court's blessing, and with assistance from local, state, and even national experts, zoning soon dominated the American legal landscape. Zoning, modified somewhat from its Euclidean origins, remains ascendant to this day, despite nagging concerns about its effect on potential newcomers, on the real estate market, and on the needs of neighboring communities.

For more than two decades, I have written about the origins and implications of the Supreme Court's decision in *Euclid v. Ambler*. During that time, I have benefited from the assistance and support of a great many people. My close association with Charles Haar — friend, mentor, and collaborator — is the chief reason why I chose land-use planning law as the focus of much of my teaching and scholarship. He "commissioned" my first exploration of the case more than twenty years ago, and we have continued to explore its intricacies and meanings ever since, in often animated conversations, and in the pages of books and articles.

One of my first law students — Bill Randle — taught me important lessons about the Cleveland region that gave birth to *Euclid v. Ambler* and about many of the area's most intriguing historical figures. Bill attended law school in the middle of a career that had already brought him fame (as a celebrated rock-and-roll disc jockey in Cleveland) and that had already been marked by high academic achievement (a doctorate in American studies from Western Reserve University, among other degrees). This student was nearly thirty years my senior, with a wealth of stories and insights about the history of his longtime home in Ohio. It was not until years after he left my classroom that I learned just what a legend Bill was, and I am sorry that his death in 2004 prevented me from showing him what a great teacher he was.

I cannot say enough about the generosity of Art Brooks, a highly respected partner at Baker Hostetler in Cleveland, who is the keeper of Newton D. Baker's zoning file. The time I have spent over the phone and in person discussing Cleveland, Baker, zoning, and history with Art has not only been pleasurable, but highly informative. Thank you, Art.

It is not often that a historian receives an unsolicited first-hand account of an important incident that took place seven decades before, but such was the case when, after publishing a short piece about *Euclid v. Ambler* in a Supreme Court historical journal, I received a letter from Milton Handler, who had served as a clerk for Justice Harlan Fiske Stone in 1926. Professor Handler provided an informative and poignant account of a nervous James Metzenbaum before and after the second oral argument in the case. I will always appreciate Professor Handler's generosity in sharing that story with me and, now, with a wider audience.

Librarians are essential partners to almost anyone engaged in serious historical research, and such was the case with this book and with my previous writings on *Euclid v. Ambler*. At the University of Richmond School of Law, I was assisted by Nancy Martin and Brandon Quarles, and at my current law school—the University of Florida Levin College of Law—Rick Donnelly, Ron Perry, Terry Rogers, and Christopher Vallandingham kept my bookshelves filled and tracked down hard-to-find primary and secondary sources. Librarians at the Cleveland office of Baker Hostetler—Al Podboy and Susan Miljenovic—were most generous with their time, as were the skilled professionals at the National Archives in Washington, D.C. My thanks also go to John Williams, the president of the Euclid Historical Society, who filled in some essential local details during my visit to the locus of the dispute, and Roy Larick, chair of the Euclid Landmark Commission, for providing me with an early zoning map of the village.

Conversations with colleagues at my home institutions and from around the country—Wade Berryhill, Joel Eisen, Mark Fenster, Jerold Kayden, Stuart Meck, and many more—informed my ideas and assisted my research. Over the past quarter century, hundreds of students have suffered through Professor Wolf's attempt to wax poetic about *Euclid v. Ambler*. I appreciate their patience and their important contributions to my thoughts about the history and implications of zoning.

The prodigious scholar, and mensch, Mel Urofsky, was the matchmaker between me and the Landmark Law series at the University Press of Kansas, and I am grateful for his confidence, support, and friendship. It has been a pleasure working with Michael Briggs on this project; his patience and perceptiveness are both appreciated. I would also like to thank those who were asked to read and comment on my original proposal and preliminary draft, particularly two leading scholars who made some important suggestions for improving the text—James Ely and Alan Weinstein.

My son, Daniel, devoted long and precious hours of otherwise free time to improving the substance and style of my presentation. I could not have asked for a more attentive editor—or son. My daughter, Rachel, and my wife, Betty, were valuable partners in this long-term project as well. I will always be grateful for their love, support, and understanding, especially when I was distracted by events and ideas that appeared on the scene long before we did.

This book is dedicated to my parents. My father, whose decision to join the family citrus and cattle business took him to Lakeland in the early 1950s, was a land developer of a different kind than H. A. Stahl. My father received no greater pleasure from his work than when he turned raw land into pasture for a herd of cattle or when he plucked a juicy orange from a grove that his father had bought many years before. When he died in 2006, he left his family a valuable legacy that cannot be measured in acres or dollar signs. My mother, always a voracious reader, taught me by example to love books, especially biographies. I hope that, after she reads this preface and then sneaks a peek at the last few pages, she decides that the chapters in between will make for a good read.

The Zoning of America

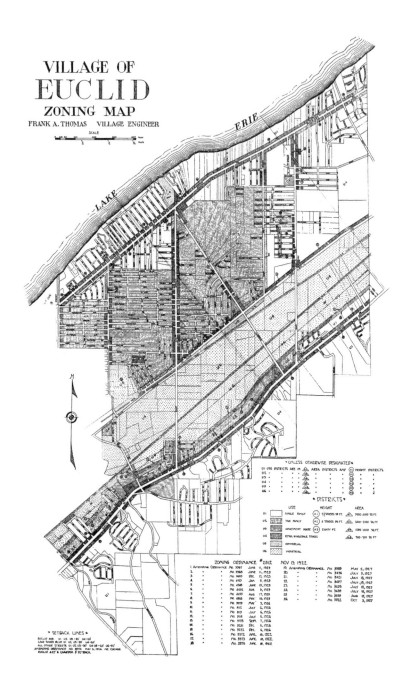

VILLAGE OF
EUCLID
ZONING MAP
FRANK A. THOMAS   VILLAGE ENGINEER

SCALE

CHAPTER I

Caught in a Snowstorm

James Metzenbaum was desperate. His train was slowed by a late January snowstorm halfway between Washington, D.C., and Cleveland, Ohio, the burgeoning midwestern metropolis where, in 1926, Metzenbaum's office was located. Metzenbaum's desperation grew out of his concern that his opposing counsel, former secretary of war Newton D. Baker, had departed from the law and the facts in the case that the two had just argued before the nation's highest tribunal, the U.S. Supreme Court. Trapped by the rules of appellate argument before the justices, and by the unwritten law of courtroom decorum, Metzenbaum, representing the Village of Euclid, Ohio, had kept silent while Baker, in the closing minutes of his presentation, seemingly shifted the momentum in the direction of Baker's client, the Ambler Realty Company.

Metzenbaum felt the need to respond immediately to Baker's argument, as the Court was about to take a break in order to decide the most recent cases in which it had heard oral arguments. Because of the inclement weather, Metzenbaum feared that he would not be able to reach his office in time to send instructions to a colleague in Washington. Metzenbaum's plan was to request permission from the Supreme Court to write a legal brief addressing the somewhat surprising points that Baker sprang upon the justices. Motivated by a feeling of responsibility to his client and to millions of other Americans who would be affected by the outcome of the case, Metzenbaum drafted a telegraph message to Chief Justice William Howard Taft, a fellow Ohioan who thirteen years before had left the office of president of the United States. The message as delivered on January 29, 1926, read in part, "AFTER REFLECTING UPON IMPORTANCE OF CAUSE AND GREAT PUBLIC INTEREST AND NOT FOR ANY MERE PERSONAL

DESIRE TO WIN FEEL CONSCIOUS DU[T]Y WOULD NOT BE FULFILLED UNLESS REQUEST IS MADE TO FILE SHORT REPLY BRIEF WITHIN SUCH TIME AS YOU MAY STIPULATE." The desperate attorney wrapped money around the telegraph message and tossed it to a worker who was shoveling freight cars out of a snowbank, shouting instructions that he hoped the worker would understand.

Five days later, the village's conscientious and very worried counsel received word from Taft that he had one week to file a reply brief and submit it to his opponent. A few weeks later, Metzenbaum learned that the justices had ordered the case to be re-briefed and re-argued, an unusual move that hinted that the Court was sharply split on the issues raised by counsel for both sides during the first round of legal briefs and oral arguments.

Final word would come in late November 1926, when the nation read about a small local government's victory over a real estate company, by a vote of six to three, in a case titled *Village of Euclid v. Ambler Realty Company*. The specific issue in the case, one that did indeed affect millions of Americans living in cities and suburbs throughout the country, concerned the validity of zoning. This relatively new method of regulating the use of land had proved quite popular since its introduction only a decade before. In the name of health and safety, and for the welfare of the general public, Euclid, like many other large and small localities in Ohio and many other states, had imposed height, area, and use limitations on the land within its borders. Metzenbaum and his prozoning allies had prevailed in the Supreme Court, despite a lower court decision declaring the practice of zoning unconstitutional and therefore invalid, Baker's ample skills in oral argument, and the Supreme Court's well-earned reputation for striking down statutes and regulations that interfered with private property and contract rights. The direct result of the Court's holding in *Euclid v. Ambler* was the continued, rapid proliferation of zoning ordinances throughout the United States. Indeed, by the middle of the twentieth century, zoning was an essential element of local government law and a practical reality faced by real estate interests in the vast majority of America's cities, towns, and suburbs. By the end of the twentieth century, the United States would be a suburban nation, as measured by population, economic power, political influence, and national self-image. For better or worse, zoning was inextricably connected to the suburbanization of the nation.

Even more important than the specific question resolved by the Supreme Court were the wider implications of the majority's decision. Although Baker and others asserted that the government had exceeded its power in passing an ordinance that potentially reduced the value of private property, six members of the Supreme Court—following the lead of many state court judges in earlier challenges to zoning—elevated the public good over private rights. For eight succeeding decades, this decision, which was based on a careful interpretation of key federal constitutional protections, would provide the legal impetus not only for comprehensive planning and zoning but also for a broad array of local, state, and federal statutes, ordinances, and regulations designed to make the nation's communities more livable, safe, healthy, aesthetically pleasing, and self-sufficient. Indeed, it is no exaggeration to say that the judicial acceptance of modern environmental law is an important legacy of *Euclid v. Ambler*.

Not all legacies of this case have been positive, for, as in *Euclid v. Ambler* itself, some land-use laws—particularly in the hands of less enlightened public officials—feature decidedly negative aspects. The most important characteristics of the underside of zoning and of other forms of land-use regulation have been the exclusion of persons and uses deemed to be "undesirable," the elimination of unwanted economic competition, the elevation of parochial over regional interests, and the indulgence in overly subjective notions of beauty and historic value. When these negative aspects are viewed through the contemporary conservative lens that is colored by a deep distrust of nearly all forms of government regulation and by a renewed devotion to private property rights, some legal commentators are anxious to consign *Euclid v. Ambler* to the waste bin of outmoded legal doctrine.

Other critics, chiefly professional planners and architects, show equal disdain for the "primitive" zoning practices upheld by the Supreme Court in 1926. Proponents of "smart growth" and "new urbanism" are quick to point an accusing finger at "Euclidean" height, area, and use zoning—particularly the segregation of residential uses—as an important contributor to urban sprawl and to our monotonous, cookie-cutter suburban landscape. In actuality, the decision in

Euclid v. Ambler makes it much easier to defend in the courts of law and public opinion those essential public regulations needed to shore up these new approaches to bettering life in the nation's cities, suburbs, and rural fringes.

Land-use controls are caught in a swirling snowstorm of ideological, political, legal, and popular controversy. Like Metzenbaum's train, zoning and planning continue to move forward, slowly but surely, propelled by the considerable impetus received from their legal point of origin—the U.S. Supreme Court in Washington, D.C.

The chapters that follow trace the background of *Euclid v. Ambler* from the founding of Cleveland in the 1790s to the reform-charged opening decades of the twentieth century. The reader will see how zoning is a quintessentially Progressive concept in both its origins and in practice even today, more than ninety years after its introduction to the American urban scene. The drama of *Euclid v. Ambler* features memorable characters, shifting scenes, and skillfully crafted sentences imbued with meaning and import. The Supreme Court opinion serves as a model of pragmatic and well-balanced Progressive jurisprudence, in contrast to several recent cases in which judges have championed private property rights over land-use and environmental regulations designed to protect public health and welfare. As detailed in the pages that follow, there are aspects of the complex legal and social legacy of *Euclid v. Ambler* that call for (and have to some extent received) correction and revision.

Chapter 2 takes the reader back to the Western Reserve in the closing years of the eighteenth century, demonstrating the curious origins of the Village of Euclid in the days of Moses Cleaveland and the Connecticut Land Company. By the early decades of the twentieth century, Cleveland and its environs were being fundamentally reshaped socially, demographically, and politically. The struggle over zoning in the Village of Euclid grew out of these seismic shifts.

Chapter 3 shows how planners, architects, and Progressive reformers, particularly those active in and influenced by the City Beautiful movement, hoped to mold responsible urban residents by shaping the urban and suburban environment. This important task required a reevaluation and redeployment of nuisance law, which had been the chief tool for reconciling discordant land uses. Unfortunately, this exceedingly confusing area of judge-made law proved quite ineffective in responding to contemporary needs and realities. This chapter recalls the struggle over the nation's first important zoning ordinance (in pre–World War I New York City) and describes the alliance of private and public sector actors (including a future president of the United States) that would design and promote zoning laws as an effective and enlightened alternative to common law controls.

As Chapter 4 demonstrates, the zoning scheme for the Village of Euclid was typical in its origins, its provisions, and in the interests that lined up in support and in opposition. When it came to the actual personalities involved in the Ambler Realty Company's legal challenge, however, the case attracted an impressive and colorful cast of characters, many of whom (from all sides of the debate over zoning) shared a commitment to Progressive reform. Baker, Metzenbaum, Judge D. C. Westenhaver, Associate Justice George Sutherland, and Alfred Bettman each left an indelible mark on the legal landscape of urban planning. This chapter also chronicles the early judicial battlegrounds over the legitimacy of this new and controversial regulatory tool.

Chapter 5 takes the *Euclid* litigation from the village's defeat in the federal trial court through two sets of briefs and oral arguments before the U.S. Supreme Court. These exchanges demonstrate the high stakes involved in a seemingly simple case of a disgruntled landowner versus an uncharitable local government. When the justices called for a rehearing, they benefited from a masterful brief written by one of the nation's leading defenders of the nascent ideas of comprehensive planning and zoning. The struggle to uphold the legitimacy of zoning in the nation's courts pitted conservative defenders of private property and contract rights against reformers who envisioned this new land-use regulatory tool as an optimal use of the state's "police power," designed to protect health and safety and to promote the general welfare.

The Court's decision in support of the Village of Euclid, the subject of Chapter 6, was penned by George Sutherland, a jurist who has long and somewhat unfairly been associated with the Court's conservative bloc, a group that opponents on the left referred to as the

Four Horsemen of the Apocalypse. Sutherland's finely honed opinion was a careful, deliberate attempt to extend the protections traditionally afforded by nuisance law to a new form of comprehensive, code-based land-use regulation. This would not be a total capitulation to the public sector, however, as Sutherland and his colleagues in the majority tempered their deference to public officials with language that decidedly limited the power of one local government to act without regard to regional needs or to the rights of individual landowners who might be treated unfairly and unreasonably.

Chapter 7 details *Euclid v. Ambler*'s immediate reception in the press, in legal scholarship, and in the Supreme Court itself. There was no widespread sense at the time that this was a revolutionary holding, despite the generally conservative tenor of the Court in the 1920s.

Chapter 8 addresses the legal legacy of *Euclid v. Ambler*. Despite the rapid proliferation of zoning and its widespread use to the dissatisfaction of some property owners in every locality, the nation's highest court, after firing one post-*Euclid* warning shot, remained nearly silent on the topic for the succeeding five decades. Filling this vacuum were decisions from state courts, as challenges to planning and zoning yielded an impressive body of creative judge-made law in the "laboratory of the states." In many instances, state judges and legislators were contending with the four troublesome seeds planted in the *Euclid* opinion itself: exclusiveness, anticompetitiveness, parochialism, and subjective aestheticism.

As the twentieth century closed, and conservative jurists again gained ascendancy on the Supreme Court, the legal battle over zoning occurred in the context of a new age of private property rights activism, as Chapter 9 demonstrates. Some observers attribute many of the nation's ills—suburban sprawl, housing segregation, and urban blight—to the kind of zoning that received the Court's blessing in *Euclid v. Ambler*. Other critics bemoan the *Euclid* court's refusal to recognize and safeguard cherished individual rights, blaming Sutherland and his brethren for shielding allegedly confiscatory and misguided environmental and land-use controls by all levels of government. The assault on the letter and spirit of *Euclid v. Ambler* takes place today in Congress and state legislatures, in the nation's courts, in academic journals, and in the popular press.

This volume closes with a return to the main players in *Euclid v. Ambler* and to the setting of the drama. Like so many communities within the zone of influence of major American cities, Euclid has been unable to resist the pressures of profound social and economic shifts that have occurred since the Roaring Twenties. The battle over the future of zoning and other forms of land-use regulation is representative of the essentially American give-and-take between private need and public benefit, between government obligations and individual rights, and between responsibility and liberty.

CHAPTER 2

Surveying and Populating the Western Reserve

The story of the American law of zoning is intimately tied to the history of metropolitan Cleveland, Ohio. Indeed, one of the most curious aspects of this nation's land-use law is that several of the leading U.S. Supreme Court decisions on the topic have involved disputes that came to the Court from communities in the Buckeye State's most populous metropolitan region. The first of these cases, *Euclid v. Ambler* (1926), is of course the subject matter of this book. At the beginning of this, the Court's seminal opinion on the legitimacy of zoning, Justice Sutherland noted that the Village of Euclid "adjoins and practically is a suburb of the City of Cleveland."

In 1976, following five decades of relative silence by the Court in the area of planning and zoning, the justices decided *City of Eastlake v. Forest City Enterprises*, in which Chief Justice Warren Burger duly noted that Eastlake, too, was "a suburb of Cleveland." In that case, the Supreme Court rejected a challenge brought by a real estate developer whose plans to build a high-rise apartment building were thwarted by a negative popular vote in a referendum. The voters had reversed the decision by city officials to approve a zoning change requested by the developer.

One year later, the Supreme Court came to the rescue of Mrs. Inez Moore, a grandmother in another suburb — East Cleveland. Almost unbelievably, Moore had been sentenced to five days in jail and a twenty-five dollar fine for violating a city ordinance by allowing her grandson (whom the city called an "illegal occupant") to live in her home without the child's parents. A sharply divided court reversed the conviction because Moore's constitutional rights to due process had been violated by a city ordinance limiting occupation of dwellings that narrowly defined the term "family."

More recently, in 2003, the Supreme Court, as it had in the

Eastlake case, rejected the pleas of a developer seeking to build multifamily housing in a city lying between Cleveland and Akron. In *City of Cuyahoga Falls v. Buckeye Community Hope Foundation*, the voters again used a referendum in an effort to undo the local government's approval of the building project. As it turned out, the referendum was eventually declared invalid under *state* law by the Ohio Supreme Court. However, the U.S. Supreme Court refused to find that the decision to allow that public vote amounted to a violation of the *federal* Constitution.

In all of these cases, judges wrestled with the difficult task of drawing the line between valid and invalid restrictions on the use of land. These and the thousands of other decisions by American courts concerning the validity of the use of zoning and planning tools are the direct result of the importance our legal and economic system has always assigned to the ownership and development of real estate. Quite often, parties who speculate in raw land are pitted in court against local governments that have imposed costly restrictions on the development of these parcels.

There is probably no region of the country that better illustrates the important connection between land speculation and the course of American history than Cleveland and its environs. All of the localities mentioned in the paragraphs above — Euclid, Eastlake, East Cleveland, and Cuyahoga Falls — are located in an area that was once known as the Western Reserve, or perhaps more accurately as the Connecticut Western Reserve. Like other eastern states, Connecticut, based on expansive language in the charter received from King Charles II in 1662, claimed ownership of lands far west of its current border. The Western Reserve got its name because this 120-mile strip (in what was to become northeastern Ohio) was the only piece of land in the Northwest Territory that was retained by the state of Connecticut in 1786 when, in exchange for the assumption of its Revolutionary War debt, that state ceded its western claims to the United States.

In 1795, fifty-eight people formed a syndicate called the Connecticut Land Company for the purpose of purchasing the vast majority of the Western Reserve. The price was $1.2 million, and proceeds from the sale were directed to the Connecticut School Fund. The following year, General Moses Cleaveland, a Revolutionary War veteran and one of the seven directors of the Connecticut Land Company, led a party of about fifty to survey and map the Western Reserve. The Reserve comprised the company's holdings along with 500,000 acres at the western end of the tract, known as the Firelands, that were set aside for Connecticut residents who had lost their homes because of fires set by British forces during the Revolutionary War. Along the way, Cleaveland negotiated a settlement of claims to the land with representatives of the Six Nations, a Native American alliance also known as the Iroquois Confederacy.

Among the group that reached the mouth of the Cuyahoga River on July 22, 1796, were the six surveyors who contributed their technical expertise to this important and ambitious venture — Augustus Porter, the principal surveyor and Cleaveland's deputy superintendent, Seth Pease, an astronomer and surveyor, along with Amos Spafford, John Milton Holey, Richard M. Stoddard, and Moses Warren. As summer turned to fall, their efforts were frustrated by faulty maps, disease, heavy rains, dangerous terrain, and dense forests. At the end of September, the disgruntled surveyors received a contract from Cleaveland and became joint owners of their own township. The name they selected for their property seemed a perfect choice for practitioners of the art and science of surveying — Euclid, after Euclid of Alexandria, a Greek mathematician who, it is believed, lived in the third century B.C.E.

The American law of zoning has long been associated with the name "Euclid"; indeed, it is common to refer to the scheme of height, area, and use classifications as "Euclidean zoning." One unfamiliar with the legal heritage of zoning would most likely presume that the adjective refers to Euclidean geometry, the set of definitions, proofs, and postulates attributed to the ancient mathematician. In fact, the notion that the mathematician and Euclidean zoning are related is basically true. It is true, however, not because zoning restrictions often appear as geometric shapes on a map, but because of the fondness the surveyors had for the "patron saint" of their profession.

As it turns out, the agreement between Cleaveland and the surveyors proved unsuccessful in two ways. First, the surveyors never lived up to their part of the bargain under which, in exchange for the price of one dollar per acre, they promised to settle a few dozen families in the township by the end of the century. Second, the contract did not keep the unhappy surveyors on the job much longer that fall, as the party exited the unfriendly wilderness in mid-October, leaving ten settlers behind to face the harsh winter.

The story of *Euclid v. Ambler* is basically a tale of two cities, or, more accurately, a city and one of its suburbs. In the decades following General Cleaveland's initial survey of the Western Reserve, it was anything but certain that the city named after the general would eclipse the township named by the surveyors. Although Cleveland was laid out in 1796 as the "principal town" of the Reserve, and one year later lots were made ready for sale, it took a few years for those lots to be settled. Indeed, by 1800, there was only one resident in the town. The hamlet grew very little in the decade following Ohio's entry into the Union in 1803 as the seventeenth state. In 1820, several of the communities in the vicinity, including the Township of Euclid (more than 35 square miles that were incorporated in 1809), contained more residents than Cleveland; but with a strong base of commerce and manufacturing, Cleveland was poised for a leap forward.

In 1825, Cleveland was established as the northern terminus of the Ohio & Erie Canal, which by 1832 ran south to Portsmouth, on the Ohio River. Increased commerce and transportation improvements reshaped Cleveland, which became a city in 1836, into a major Great Lakes port by the mid-1840s. Another important change transformed Cleveland forever — significant immigration from Germany and Ireland. In the years before the Civil War, railroads helped prepare the region for manufacturing growth, including the Cleveland, Painesville & Ashtabula Railroad, which ran through Euclid on its way to Erie, Pennsylvania, in 1852.

The Civil War completed the city's transformation from commerce to industry, and the city's landscape featured dozens of oil refineries and several rolling mills serviced by five railroad lines. Cleveland's immigrant population continued to climb. In 1860, 43,000 Clevelanders occupied the city's 7 square miles. The city boundaries spread to 12 square miles by 1867, and in 1870 the city's population had mushroomed to over 92,000, more than 40 percent of whom were foreign-born. At the same time, residents of communities outside the city limits formed villages such as the first incarnation of East Cleveland (1866) and Glenville (1870). In 1877, residents of Euclid Township decided to incorporate as a village; but, upon reconsideration, they rescinded the incorporation the following year. By the end of the century, many of these independent municipalities had been absorbed into an expanding Cleveland, including the first East Cleveland in 1891 and Glenville four years later.

Cleveland proper was the home to some of the nation's wealthiest industrialists, including John D. Rockefeller, who controlled nine-tenths of the nation's oil refining capacity and whose mansion was located on stately Euclid Avenue. Beginning in the closing decades of the nineteenth century, those blocks of the street running eastward from downtown were nicknamed Millionaire's Row. With the influx of impoverished immigrants from southern and eastern Europe during this same period, the city was a textbook example of social stratification. By 1890, three-quarters of the city's 260,000 residents were immigrants or the children of immigrants. At the same time, African Americans constituted a little over 1 percent of the population.

In the new century, Cleveland's population kept burgeoning. By 1910, it was the sixth largest American city, with over 560,000 residents. Cleveland was an industrial juggernaut that turned out iron and steel manufacturing, ships, and automobiles. Skilled and unskilled workers competed for space in apartment buildings, row houses, and one-family homes divided into several units. In fact, the city faced a housing crisis. Poorer denizens occupied the central city, and middle-class residents lived in streetcar neighborhoods. Complicating matters was a slowly growing African American population (reaching several thousand in the years before World War I) that attracted increased ill-will from white Clevelanders.

While World War I and strict federal laws brought an end to immigration from Hungary, Poland, Russia, and southern Italy, African Americans from the South began to fill the labor gap. Their numbers grew steadily to over 30,000 by 1920, as part of the Great Migration to the North. At the same time these newcomers were squeezed into poor, central city neighborhoods, wealthier Clevelanders began to abandon Millionaire's Row. Even local politics were becoming hard to tolerate for the city's more affluent elements, as evidenced by the May Day Riots in 1919. Violence broke out when the socialist leader Charles Ruthenberg (later a leading American communist) organized a parade in protest of the imprisonment of Eugene V. Debs for opposing American participation in World War I. The federal district court judge who had sentenced Debs to a ten-year prison sentence one year before the riots—D. C. Westenhaver—was destined to play a key role in Euclid's zoning story a few years later. When the violence was over, two were dead, forty were injured, and more than one hundred were arrested.

The older suburbs established in the closing decades of the nineteenth century along horse-drawn railway lines had with regularity been absorbed into Cleveland proper by annexation. In the new century, residents of some suburbs, disturbed by the perceived harms of the city, began to resist Cleveland's efforts to grow. Many middle- and upper-class residents seeking a better life outside the city limits would find their prayers answered in 1905, when the brothers Oris Paxson (O. P.) and Mantis James (M. J.) Van Sweringen, two budding real estate developers who were only in their twenties, started to acquire land to the east of the city, in Shaker Heights. One of the Van Sweringens' biographers, Herbert H. Harwood, Jr., provided this description of the "gritty environment" in Cleveland that produced the market for a new kind of suburban community:

All those steel mills and refineries along the Cuyahoga River sat next to the city's heart, spewing out dark clouds of varied colors, odors, and chemical content; beyond them on three sides were plants turning out all manner of industrial and consumer products. And moving through it all were hundreds of coal-fired steam locomotives and lake freighters, all adding their own rich mix of black bituminous smoke. Then there were the people—those immigrants and their cloistered neighborhoods, destabilizing property values. And finally there was the delicate problem of odor—put more bluntly, the stench. The industrial air and the unwashed human bodies were not the only problem. Horses still moved all the goods and many of the people around the city; thousands of them and their inevitable by-products were all dumped into the streets.

While the Vans (as the nearly inseparable pair would come to be called) would strike out in their first attempt to tap the new suburban market in Lakewood, to the west of the city, they were much more successful when they turned their attention eastward to a large tract of land that was once part of the North Union Shaker community.

The Shakers, an ascetic, celibate sect, farmed their communal holdings beginning in the 1820s. The community sold its land in 1892 to investors from Cleveland who renamed the area Shaker Heights and hoped to create housing for suburbanites. In 1905, the Van Sweringens acquired options on some of the lots, which they then sold at a profit. Soon after, with financial backers in place, the brothers were set to develop the entire tract, which stretched for several thousand acres. They envisioned a community for families from the upper- and upper-middle classes, and, following the model established by neighborhoods such as Baltimore's Roland Park, they put in place architectural controls and legal protections, such as restrictive deed provisions, designed to ensure high real estate values. Quick and direct transportation for the residents to the business center of Cleveland, preferably under the control of the developers themselves, was a key component of the plans to develop Shaker Heights Village, which was incorporated in 1911.

The Van Sweringens' desire to create a direct interurban railroad route between Shaker Heights and Public Square in Cleveland brought them into contact with the owners of the New York, Chicago & St. Louis Railroad Company, known from the line's opening in 1882 as the Nickel Plate Road. Regarding the nickname, Harwood, in *Invisible Giants: The Empires of Cleveland's Van Sweringen Brothers*, explained:

> One legend about the name of the Nickel Plate has it that William H. Vanderbilt said "I wouldn't buy that damned railroad if it were nickel-plated." Another is that it came from a corruption of the company's initials, "NYCL." But most historians give the credit to the Norwalk, Ohio, *Chronicle*, which reportedly referred to the line during its construction as "the great New York and St. Louis nickel-plated railroad." At the time, Norwalk had hoped the railroad would build through the town and locate its shops there.

Moreover, the official name was misleading, as the 523-mile single line ran between Buffalo and Chicago, not New York City and St. Louis.

It has long been believed that the Nickel Plate, which followed the same route as Vanderbilt's New York Central Railroad between Buffalo and Chicago, was funded by investors who speculated that Vanderbilt or one of his competitors would buy out the new entry into the market. If so, their plans came to fruition when, a few days after the Nickel Plate started to run, Vanderbilt took the bait by purchasing a majority interest of the new line, which ran freight, not passengers, between the two industrial cities.

Vanderbilt's domination of the rail business in that part of the country was free from government interference for a few decades. However, when federal antitrust laws were toughened by the passage of the Clayton Act in 1914, change was in the air. When New York Central's president received word that the Justice Department was concerned about one company controlling so many parallel routes, the search was on for suitable buyers for the Nickel Plate, buyers who would not pose a serious competitive threat. In 1916, the Van Sweringens, who had expressed an interest in acquiring a three-quarter mile stretch of the line's right-of-way in downtown Cleveland, ended up purchasing a majority interest in the entire Nickel Plate with much-needed financing from a local bank.

Anxious to maintain their control over their new company with the least financial exposure, the Vans used an elaborate form of ownership, the holding company, which the brothers employed over the succeeding decade and a half to create a massive railroad empire. They achieved their more immediate goal—creating a direct link from Shaker Heights to central Cleveland—in the spring of 1920. Over the next ten years, the suburb's population would mushroom from 1,616 to more than 17,793. In 1931, the Vans' innovative community would become a city.

Another smaller, high-end, residential community, Ambler Heights, was developed in Cleveland's eastern suburbs at roughly the same time as Shaker Heights. This 350-acre development was in the southwest corner of Cleveland Heights (incorporated as a village in 1901) and only a few miles away from Shaker Heights. The development was named after Dr. Nathan Hardy Ambler, a dentist who amassed a small fortune plying his trade during the California Gold Rush and set up a practice in Cleveland in 1852, where he increased his wealth by speculating in real estate. Upon the dentist's death in

1888, Dr. Ambler's adopted son, Daniel Criswell, and nephew, Judge William E. Ambler, began marketing Ambler Heights, conveniently located adjacent to a street railway line and to the Euclid Club, a private golf club that operated until 1914. Criswell and Judge Ambler, like the Vans, employed deed restrictions to ensure the construction of large, single-family dwellings on spacious lots. Many of the Cleveland area's leading business figures secured the services of leading architects to build beautiful homes in a tranquil, wooded setting.

At the time that many of Cleveland's elite were settling Shaker Heights, Ambler Heights, and other residential enclaves in the eastern suburbs, the once-grand blocks of Euclid Avenue were being converted to commercial and other nonresidential uses. From its western terminus in Public Square, Euclid Avenue ran directly east through the city before taking a turn to the northeast along Lakeview Cemetery (a short distance from Ambler Heights), through the second East Cleveland (which was incorporated as a village in 1895 and became a city in 1911), back through the northeastern edge of Cleveland, and into and beyond the Village of Euclid, which was reincorporated in 1903.

The automobile held the promise of continued rapid growth of new, independent suburbs and of established communities within easy reach of Cleveland. But the mass production of vehicles with internal combustion engines that ran on gasoline also meant that it would be easier for factories to relocate from the central city and move their goods and materials by truck in addition to, or in the place of, rail. Moreover, those new suburban factories would need to house their workers nearby, most likely in apartment houses from which the residents could take rapid transit or autobuses.

Euclid was at a crossroads, literally and figuratively. Would its landscape be dominated by industry and commerce spreading eastward from Cleveland along the New York Central and Nickel Plate lines and along the direct traffic routes such as Euclid Avenue? Or would the village be able to maintain its predominantly residential character by attracting the new, deed-restricted subdivisions used to shape Shaker Heights and Ambler Heights? The answer depended in large part on changes in the laws regulating land use that swept the nation in the 1920s.

CHAPTER 3

On the Road to Zoning

As with any other major legal innovation, the development of the American form of zoning as typified by the Village of Euclid's 1922 ordinance can be attributed to several complementary factors. The chief elements that contributed to the adoption of the specific zoning ordinance that received the Supreme Court's blessing in *Euclid v. Ambler* were (1) the shortcomings of traditional, common-law methods for regulating land use; (2) the growing influence of planning ideas and the planning profession in urban America; (3) the importation of zoning ideas from New York City and from the model act circulated by the U.S. Department of Commerce; and (4) the prevailing social and political ethos of the Progressive Era, during which great faith was placed in expert-based governmental solutions to social and economic problems.

By the close of the nineteenth century, American judges and lawyers, building upon the foundation of centuries of Anglo-American law contained primarily in judicial opinions and in treatises written by widely respected legal experts, had developed five important methods of addressing or even anticipating (and thereby avoiding) conflicts between competing property owners over the use and abuse of land: private nuisance, trespass to land, public nuisance, defeasible fees, and restrictive covenants. Although these legal concepts are conceptually related, each is technically a discrete area of English and American property law that over the course of hundreds of years had developed its own set of rules and operating principles. To many observers, no one method, indeed not even any combination of these five methods, proved up to the important task of protecting landowners from the negative impacts of their neighbors' use of land while respecting all landowners' important constitutional rights. At this point, it will be helpful to review the chief shortcomings of each of these prezoning forms of land-use regulation, paying special attention to Ohio's legal experience.

Private nuisance is a tort action typically brought by one landowner against a neighboring or nearby owner who unreasonably and substantially interferes with the first owner's use and enjoyment of real property. In a 1905 case from Cincinnati, for example, Bernard Klumper, the owner of a two-story brick home in which his family had resided for ten years, sought to prevent Theodore Vogelgesang, the owner of an adjoining lot, from operating a "horseshoing shop" on the first floor of his own two-story brick dwelling. Citing the noises, smells, and noxious odors that emanated from this type of business, Klumper requested that the court order Vogelsgang to shut down the blacksmith operation. Judge Hoffheimer of the Superior Court of Cincinnati denied the relief sought by Klumper, refusing to find that the operation of the blacksmith shop "work[ed] a substantial inconvenience and discomfort to the plaintiff [Klumper] in the use and enjoyment of his property." Although a visit to the site of the dispute confirmed the presence of noise and smells, as well as cinders cast on the Klumper property, the judge noted that the character of the once-residential street was "gradually undergoing a change, and there are now numerous shops and mercantile houses in the vicinity." Indeed, close by Klumper's house were a grocery, laundry, saloon, and similar commercial uses. The bottom line was that Judge Hoffheimer could not "say that a *substantial* and *material injury is worked or can be worked to an ordinary person willing to put up with the ordinary things in city life.*" Klumper could not carry the heavy burden of demonstrating a "strong and pressing necessity" for getting rid of the blacksmith shop next door, and this proved fatal to his case and to his efforts to maintain the residential character of this urban neighborhood.

Trespass to land, another tort action, is closely related to and often confused with private nuisance. The key to recovering under a trespass theory is the physical invasion of another's property without the owner's consent. Even though the slightest invasion, even an accidental one, can give rise to a successful lawsuit in trespass, in the early twentieth century, and even to this day, courts have wrestled with the difficult task of deciding whether landowners whose buildings crack, break, and suffer other physical damage because of the activities of others should be able to bring trespass actions in the *absence* of an actual invasion. Thus, trespass is not an effective device for regulating competing land uses in the same general vicinity.

When property owners conduct activities on their lands that actually pose a threat to the health and safety of the community as a whole, local governments, wielding their traditional police power, can prosecute the wrongdoers for conducting an illegal public nuisance. However, it is not often that residential, commercial, and even industrial users cross the high threshold of actual public harm. For example, when Ashland, Ohio, passed an ordinance in 1925 making it unlawful "for any person, corporation or partnership, to conduct a junk yard within the city limits," the court of common pleas struck down the local law, noting that "the legislature or the city council may not under the guise of protecting the public interests, arbitrarily interfere with private business and interpose unusual and unnecessary restrictions upon lawful occupations or business." Because the court deemed the question of what constituted a public nuisance to be a judicial and not a legislative matter, the ordinance was "declared invalid, void and of no effect."

In the late nineteenth and early twentieth centuries, real estate developers in several metropolitan areas experimented with a form of property ownership known as the "defeasible" or "qualified" or "limited" fee. Unlike the much more common "fee simple absolute" title, which placed no restrictions on the new owner, the defeasible fee had been used for centuries by owners to control the use of property even after its transfer to churches or government entities. It was not uncommon for owners to stipulate that, should the property no longer be used for religious, school, or other limited purposes, title would revert to the owner or the owner's heirs. The experimental use of the defeasible fee to ensure that subsequent owners in the subdivision maintained certain important features (setbacks, residential uses, and the like) ultimately failed, as courts were hesitant to order owners to forfeit their properties (including buildings and other permanent improvements) as punishment for violating the limitations inherent in the title.

In the 1890s, for example, Thomas Marshall inserted language into the deeds for seven of the nine lots in an Akron subdivision providing that, should the purchasers build or maintain any structure within 50 feet of the street, ownership of the properties would revert to his heirs or assigns. Decades later, Marshall's heirs attempted to reclaim two of the lots upon which sat a Christian Science church with a front porch extending to within 47 feet of the street. The court of appeals affirmed the decision of the trial court and refused to grant the heirs the relief they sought. The judges were not convinced that to interpret the deed so as to create a defeasible fee and thereby raise the possibility of forfeiture for even a minor infraction was consistent with Marshall's original intent. Instead, the court of appeals chose to construe the provision as a restrictive covenant, deciding to deny relief to the heirs in the light of the fact that they had failed to enforce the provision against other offending owners for more than thirty-five years.

As early as the opening decades of the 1800s, one popular method for maintaining the residential character and the aesthetic amenities of the new communities that were established on the outskirts of American cities was the inclusion of restrictive covenants in the deeds that passed title from the real estate developer to each new homeowner. These contractual provisions were designed to prevent not only the first purchaser but also subsequent homebuyers from building structures too close to their neighbors or to the street, from using their property for commercial purposes, and from otherwise disturbing the pleasant, residential character of the neighborhood. It was also not uncommon for suburban developers to include racial and religious restrictions in the set of restrictive covenants, designed to keep out a wide range of "undesirables."

There was no guarantee that courts would enforce these covenants against landowners, particularly when the landowner who was accused of violating the restriction was not one of the original parties to the covenant agreement. In a 1900 case from Toledo, for example, the circuit court refused to allow one lot owner (Hermina Russell) to enforce a restrictive covenant that forbade the construction of structures in the neighborhood closer than 20 feet from the street line against the adjoining property owner (Oliver Harpel), who had commenced construction of a house, parts of which (the porch and a bay windows) were within 10 and 15 feet of the street. The developer routinely included the restrictions in the deeds that he transferred to the *original* purchasers of these two and other lots in the neighborhood. Harpel purchased his lot from one of those original purchasers (E. W. Tolerton), but Tolerton failed to include the covenant language in his deed to the new owner. That factor seemed to work in Harpel's favor, along with the reality that Harpel had already spent several hundred dollars in the construction of his home. Moreover, many of the homes already constructed in the same block were positioned closer than 20 feet to the street, including the house on the other side of Russell's lot, which was set back only 14 feet. The judges concluded that to allow Russell to prevent Harpel's construction "would be unjust and inequitable and unconscionable."

As explained in Chapter 2, in the early twentieth century, large-scale "community builders" such as the Van Sweringens and the Amblers employed deed restrictions in creating their suburban, high-end communities of Shaker Heights and Ambler Heights. Based on the state of the law at the time, there was certainly no guarantee that state courts would enforce those restrictions against an owner who chose not to comply. In fact, it would not be until 1929, in a case brought by a Shaker Heights landowner named Dixon against the Van Sweringen Company, that the Supreme Court of Ohio would recognize the general enforceability of a set of substantially similar deed restrictions. Those restrictions were imposed on a wide number of purchasers, subject to exceptions. In affirming the lower court, Justice Robert H. Day wrote:

> Until some concrete case arises, showing that public policy has been violated, we see no reason for denying the right of these parties to contract between themselves, the result of such contracts up to date being, as we are advised by the arguments of counsel, to create a highly exclusive and valuable residential district. Not only do these restrictive agreements operate in favor of the original grantor, but, where there is an improvement scheme covering an entire allotment, as here, with reference to which lots in the tract are sold and conveyed by deeds containing restrictive covenants, the grantee of one lot may enforce these covenants against the grantee of another lot and also against the grantor when the rights of the grantee are invaded.

Before the 1920s, however, in Ohio and elsewhere, the legal footing of these neighborhood restrictions was much less secure.

Today, developers of residential subdivisions continue to employ, and neighborhood associations attempt to enforce, restrictive covenants (along with easements and equitable "servitudes") covering an ever-expanding list of topics, including but not limited to architectural styles, exterior colors, roof shingle materials, landscaping, fencing, mailboxes, vehicle parking, tool sheds, basketball goals, signs, and flagpoles. Nevertheless, since the Supreme Court announced its holding in *Euclid v. Ambler*, zoning controls—authorized by state legislation and enforced chiefly by local elected and appointed officials—are the primary means for segregating incompatible uses and protecting landowners from the harmful effects of their neighbors.

This solution to the inadequacies of common-law controls—governmental regulation—was so simple that one wonders why it took until the second decade of the twentieth century for comprehensive zoning to appear. First, we must recall that America had only recently turned the corner of urbanization. As Richard Hofstadter noted in his groundbreaking work, *The Age of Reform*:

> From 1860 to 1910, towns and cities sprouted up with miraculous rapidity all over the United States. Large cities grew into great metropolises, small towns grew into large cities, and new towns sprang into existence on vacant land. While the rural population almost doubled during this half century, the urban population multiplied almost seven times. Places with more than 50,000 inhabitants increased in number from 16 to 109. The larger cities of the Middle West grew wildly. Chicago more than doubled its population in the single decade from 1880 to 1890, while the Twin Cities trebled theirs, and others like Detroit, Milwaukee, Columbus, and Cleveland increased from sixty to eighty per cent.

The urge to impose some semblance of order on urban chaos helps to explain the widespread support for planning and zoning.

Second, while state encouragement of private enterprise is as old as the Republic, it was not until the closing years of the nineteenth century that the idea of significant government tampering with "free" enterprise was accepted, and even encouraged, by many politicians, judges, and social scientists. As the new century dawned, even the more conservative members of the Supreme Court were beginning to adjust to the idea that some experimentation under the rubric of the police power was permitted, if not desirable, despite allegations that cherished constitutional liberties were being violated.

The Supreme Court had begun to develop an incremental, experience- and fact-centered approach to evaluating the legitimacy of comprehensive legislative attempts to regulate the use and ownership of real property. In fact, one careful study by Professor Gordon Hylton found that, during the first two decades of the twentieth century, the Court consistently "found that the police power was sufficiently broad to warrant restrictions on the use of land, even when they eliminated existing uses and imposed severe economic loss on landowners." Included in the Court's caseload during this period were unsuccessful challenges brought against height restrictions (Boston), rent control ordinances (New York City and Washington, D.C.), a burial ban (San Francisco), a brothel district (New Orleans), and land-use restrictions on dairies and stables (St. Louis and Little Rock), billiard and pool halls (South Pasadena), brick manufacturers (Los Angeles), and billboards (Chicago and St. Louis).

Another key factor in explaining the development, ascendancy, and widespread acceptance of zoning was that the Progressive Era witnessed the triumph of American professionalism, a movement that, beginning in the 1870s, had recast the nation's educational and economic landscape. Urban planners — like lawyers, physicians, architects, university professors, social workers, and other professionals — established a national organization, developed specialized curricula, produced a code of ethics, and practiced their skills in order to better society. According to a leading historian on the subject, Burton Bledstein, the professional "excavated nature for its principles, its theoretical rules, thus transcending mechanical procedures, individual cases, miscellaneous facts, technical information, and instrumental applications." Notable figures such as Frederick Jackson Turner (in history), Oliver Wendell Holmes, Jr. (in law), and Jane Addams (in social work), "attempted to define a total coherent system of necessary knowledge within a precise territory, to control the intrinsic relationships of their subject by making it a scholarly as well as an applied science."

Planning certainly had left its imprint on Ohio and Cleveland in the opening years of the twentieth century. Chicago's World's Columbian Exposition in 1893 — commemorating the 400th anniversary of Columbus's first voyage to the New World — is often identified with good reason as the starting place for a discussion of planning in America. The exposition's "White City," planned and directed by the architect Daniel H. Burnham in the beaux arts architectural style, created a visual image that would become identified with the City Beautiful movement. That national movement, designed to dramatically change the urban landscape, was a complement to urban reforms in the Progressive Era.

In 1902, Burnham took his vision on the road — to Ohio. The governor named Burnham and two others to the Group Plan Commission. A fellow member, Arnold Brunner, recalled that "the problem presented to us was to devise a plan which would combine in some harmonious manner Cleveland's public buildings and provide them a proper setting and approaches." The Group Plan was presented in 1903, and it received a great deal of positive attention throughout the nation. Over the succeeding three decades, much of the plan's vision — beaux arts, classical architecture with uniform building height — was realized by the construction of major structures such as the federal and county courthouses, the city hall, and the public library, with a wide mall in the center.

Brunner's recollection occurred in a presentation that he made in June 1916, during the Eighth National Conference on City Planning held in Cleveland. The initial conference, held in 1909 in Washington, D.C., assembled for the first time some of the nation's leading experts to share ideas about the budding profession of planning. In his insightful study, *Zoned American*, Seymour Toll explained:

> It was a genuine beginning in that it was the first time together for the specific purpose of exchanging views on the problems and prospects of city planning. The subject was still so vaguely outlined and fragmented that it would be more accurate to call it a congeries of interests having something to do with the development of cities rather than a well-defined, let alone a systematic, field of knowledge. Yet a crystallizing idea was at work, for although the conferees were sometimes talking about unconnect-

ed things and often on very different levels, they had at least and at last made a serious effort to have common discourse.

That same year, Burnham and Edward H. Bennett presented their landmark Plan of Chicago, envisioning an integrated system of lakefront parks, streets, private and public buildings, and a metropolitan greenbelt that inspired city planning for decades to come. One year later, in 1910, the federal government got in on the act when President William Howard Taft charged the newly created National Commission on Fine Arts with implementing the McMillan Plan of 1901–1902, an ambitious scheme for the nation's capital that Burnham helped shape. That comprehensive plan, an extension of the beaux arts, neoclassical form of the White City, was a modern reworking of Pierre L'Enfant's original vision for the capital city. In *The City Beautiful Movement*, William H. Wilson wrote, "What observers [of the McMillan Plan] saw was a grand architectonic production, a confirmation of the role of civic design in city planning."

Over the next few years, planning advocates, many of whom were trained in law or architecture, sought to put into action some of the ideas discussed in the annual conferences and other fora. The central figure in Ohio planning was Alfred Bettman, a Harvard-educated son of German-Jewish immigrants. He returned home to Cincinnati from law school in 1898 and began a long record of service to the bar, the city, the state, and the nation. Bettman was a major force behind the drafting of Ohio's legislation in 1915 authorizing local governments to create municipal planning commissions; the Woman's City Club of Cincinnati complemented Bettman's efforts with effective lobbying efforts. While other Ohio cities took advantage of this new tool, Cincinnati's political leaders balked at a provision mandating a two-thirds vote from the city council to depart from the city plan. Instead, the mayor appointed an unofficial commission as a less satisfactory substitute.

In the pages of the *National Municipal Review* in 1917, Bettman reported that, at a meeting of that commission, one of the members raised the question of the constitutionality of newer planning controls. Banning nuisance-like industries from certain parts of town and limiting the heights of buildings was one thing, some conservative voices argued; creating residential enclaves was something much different. In a prescient passage, the lawyer-planner who would play a key role in the *Euclid v. Ambler* litigation wrote:

> I believe that districting and other features of a city planning scheme will generally be upheld by the courts, when the legislation is the result of a comprehensive and scientific study. For the courts have really gone no further than to exclude districting or other regulations for purely esthetic purposes, or the arbitrary selection of a district or zone. A comprehensive city plan, based on a thorough, expert study and upon the promotion of the health, safety, and comfort of the whole community, will surely sooner or later — and probably sooner — be upheld by the supreme court of the United States as a modern form of the regulation of the use of private property for the promotion of general public safety, health, comfort, and welfare; especially as it can be demonstrated, if the ordinance is based upon a thorough study of the situation, that the effect of a city planning ordinance will tend to be toward the stabilizing of values, rather than of destroying or diminishing values.

Bettman was an active participant in several National Conferences on City Planning beginning in 1913, contributing important insights in the heated discussions regarding the constitutionality of planning controls, particularly the "zoning" district approach taken in New York City. He was also active in the other national organizations formed by the practitioners of the new profession, such as the American City Planning Institute (founded in 1917).

Zoning did not appear overnight in American cities. Piecemeal public regulations on the use of land designed to protect urban residents from fire, smoke, and other hazards date back to colonial times. Building and tenement codes were not rarities at the dawn of the twentieth century; often they were implemented in response to muckraking exposés of the horrors experienced by denizens of low-income neighborhoods, such as David Riis's startling photographic exploration of *How the Other Half Lives: Studies among the Tenements of New York* (1890). Variations on the theme of dividing a municipality into districts based on the uses permitted and forbidden within each district could be found in locations such as Los Angeles as early as 1909 and even earlier in German cities such as Frankfurt-on-the-Main. Yet, the specific form of districting to which Bettman was most likely referring, and the form that dominates the American legal landscape today, can be traced to a specific place at a specific time: New York City in 1916. For it was in July of that year that the New York City Board of Estimate and Apportionment, by a vote of 15 to 1, adopted the Building Zone Plan, better known as the 1916 Zoning Resolution.

In 1913, Manhattan Borough President George McAneny addressed the Board of Estimate and proposed the formation of a Height of Buildings Commission to explore the concept of dividing the entire city into districts or zones. McAneny noted the "increasing evil" caused by closing off access to light and air and the dangers posed by traffic on the streets and by fire. The last peril was fresh in the minds of New Yorkers, as only two years before, on March 25, 1911, 146 workers in the Triangle Shirtwaist Factory, most of them Jewish and Italian immigrant teenagers, lost their lives in a horrendous fire that spread quickly through the Asch Building near Washington Square. The commission would be chaired by Edward M. Bassett, widely recognized today as the "father of zoning."

Bassett practiced law in Buffalo for several years before returning to his native Brooklyn, whose voters elected him to Congress. He served but one term, choosing instead to pursue public service on the state and local levels. While a member of the New York Public Service Commission, to which he was appointed by then-governor Charles Evans Hughes (a friend from Columbia Law School), Bassett got a first-hand view of city planning innovations in Germany. Back in America, Bassett became an active participant in the National Conference on City Planning.

The New York City commission that Bassett chaired spent several months investigating a wide range of issues and presented a 300-page report on December 23, 1913 (the 1913 Report) that discussed the problems posed by skyscrapers; surveyed land-use controls at home, in Canada, and in Europe (especially Germany); and argued that zoning was constitutional.

Three more years of investigations, negotiations, and struggles would ensue before the 1916 Zoning Resolution became law. One important element was secured in 1914, when the New York legislature amended the city's charter to allow for the implementation of zoning.

Because New York's ordinance stands as the basic model for American zoning during its formative period (roughly 1916–1930), it has been the subject of many historical treatments. Professor Raphaël Fischler has provided a helpful summary of the "well known story" of the forces behind the drafting and adoption of the resolution:

> The Committee on Building Heights and the Commission on Building Districts and Restrictions had worked under heavy pressure from real estate and business owners who were anxious to put an end to the damages wrought by uncontrolled development. Office buildings in the financial district were losing their light and air to higher and bulkier skyscrapers, while fancy retail stores on Fifth Avenue were seeing their high-class status eroded by the intrusion of tall garment factories. The members of the two commissions—among whom were planning pioneers and advocates such as Edward M. Bassett, Robert H. Whitten, and George B. Ford—built on the intellectual and technical foundation laid by Benjamin Marsh, Lawrence Veiller, and other reformers who had fought to reduce the congestion of the population of Manhattan. The commissions' work represented the latest and most ambitious efforts of municipalities to control the design of buildings and the use of land. . . . But the New York City ordinance went further: it was the first comprehensive zoning ordinance, that is, the first ordinance that applied both use and bulk restrictions to the entire municipality.

Within a year, the ideas debated and tools spawned in New York City would be directly transported 460 miles to the west in metropolitan Cleveland, thanks to one key participant in the commission's work—Robert H. Whitten.

His work completed in New York, Whitten moved to Cleveland, where for the next four years his ample experience with planning, traffic, and legislative drafting were in high demand. William Randle has reported that Whitten worked on zoning ordinances for the suburbs of Lakewood, East Cleveland, and Cleveland Heights and "designed a comprehensive outer parkway system that dramatically enhanced the value of suburban areas." Although he hit a dead end when trying to convince Cleveland officials to jump on the zoning bandwagon, he left an indelible legal imprint in the metropolitan region.

Whitten would also work on ordinances in Columbus, Providence, Dallas, and Atlanta (featuring a racial component until the ordinance was struck down by the Georgia Supreme Court). But he was not the only missionary who spread the good word about zoning in cities and suburbs throughout the nation. By 1921, only five years after the passage of New York's resolution, roughly twenty states had authorized some or all municipalities to pass comprehensive zoning ordinances.

The number of states with enabling acts would double over the next decade, and the number of localities with zoning ordinances actually in place would grow exponentially. A major force for fostering and supplying important model legislation for the growth on the state and local levels was the U.S. Department of Commerce, headed up by then-secretary Herbert Hoover, the engineer who played a key role in the European relief effort following World War I and who was destined to serve as U.S. president during the beginnings of the Great Depression. Hoover was interested in encouraging homeownership, which in his vision would be good for business and society. He was also concerned about the harms to urban residents posed by the absence of city planning. To that end, he created two committees, one to draft a state housing code, the other to draft model zoning and planning acts. John Gries from Harvard's business school, whom Hoover appointed to head up the new Division of Building and Housing within the department's Bureau of Standards, was charged with filling the membership of these two committees.

Hoover solicited names from various national organizations, such as the U.S. Chamber of Commerce, the National Association of Real Estate Boards, and the National Conference on City Planning, to serve on the second body, which came to be known as the Advisory Committee on City Planning and Zoning. Among the notable experts who chose to serve were Frederick Law Olmsted, Jr., the landscape architect who worked hard to promote the McMillan Plan for Washington, D.C.; Morris Knowles, a civil engineer representing the Chamber of Commerce; Nelson P. Lewis; the chief engineer of New York City's Board of Estimate; Lawrence Veiller, a noted housing expert who worked on New York's 1913 Plan; and the father of zoning himself, Edward M. Bassett. The last four served on a subcommittee that produced the Standard State Zoning Enabling Act (SZEA). On September 15, 1922, after several drafts, the Department of Commerce circulated several thousand copies of a preliminary version. Another version was published in December, and the final version followed in May 1924, with a revised edition in 1926. Only the September version of the SZEA would arrive in Euclid, Ohio, in time to have an impact on the formation of the village's first zoning ordinance. In the meantime, litigants in state courts in Ohio and other states were struggling mightily over the validity of this new creature called "zoning."

Zoning as an American legal institution is readily identified with the Progressive Era. As the twentieth century dawned, Progressive lawmakers — Republicans, Democrats, and members of third parties alike — offered a panoply of programs designed to reform the nation's political processes, to improve working conditions for American laborers and living conditions for urban denizens, to check the unbridled expansion of monopolies and trusts, and to outlaw unfair trade practices and excessive rates. Although there were certainly divisions within the various groups whose members identified themselves as "Progressive," one theme that permeated their reform efforts was a strong belief that the talents of experts drawn from the newly professionalized ranks — chiefly economists, political scientists, social workers, lawyers, and teachers — should be harnessed by governments at all levels to help individual Americans reach their full potential.

In many ways, zoning is a quintessential Progressive concept. Many of the key components are present: the reliance on experts to craft and enforce a regulatory scheme; the belief that a pleasant environment would foster healthy, responsible citizens; and the trust in decentralized control, a belief in the idea epitomized in Frederic Howe's *The City: The Hope of Democracy*. But there was another sentiment shared by many active in the Progressive movement that was underlying zoning and that contributed to its approval and popularity in the conservative climate of the 1920s: a decidedly negative view of the immigrants, particularly southern and eastern Europeans, who from the 1880s to the mid-1920s poured into America's cities in "alarming" numbers.

The very shape and political structure of many American metropolitan areas were influenced in large part by the influx of "undesirable" newcomers. As Sam Bass Warner, Jr., detailed in relation to Boston and its environs in *Streetcar Suburbs*, and as expanded upon by Kenneth Jackson in *Crabgrass Frontier*, the annexation movement lost momentum in the final years of the nineteenth century. This allowed for the growth of suburbs that ringed America's burgeoning cities.

The new Americans were the catalyst, if not the cause of suburbanization. Warner found that "the new suburbs offered ever new areas of homogeneous middle class settlement," while Jackson observed that the "newcomers were associated with and were often regarded as the cause of intemperance, vice, urban bossism, crime, and radicalism of all kinds. And as the central city increasingly became the home of the disadvantaged, the number of white commuters rose markedly." Unlike New Dealers and post–World War II liberals who drew political support from inner-city residents, many Progressives viewed the immigrant, in alliance with the manipulative urban machine, as a barrier to effective political and social reform. The homogeneous suburb, populated by middle-class homeowners, offered the hope of good government and local control. One such suburb, Euclid, would employ the new tool of zoning in an attempt to maintain its status as a residential haven in an industrializing region.

CHAPTER 4

From Gotham to Hamlet

Zoning Comes to Euclid

The zoning scheme for the Village of Euclid was not unusual in its origins, in its provisions, or in the arguments pro and con that it provoked. When it came to the actual personalities involved in the Ambler Realty Company's challenge, however, the *Euclid* case attracted an impressive, colorful, and unique cast of characters, many of whom (on both sides) shared a commitment to Progressive reform causes. The *Euclid v. Ambler* controversy involved such national notables as Newton D. Baker (counsel for Ambler Realty), Alfred Bettman (who contributed a timely and influential *amicus* brief), and Justice George Sutherland (author of the Supreme Court's majority opinion), as well as local figures of note such as James Metzenbaum (counsel for the Village of Euclid), Judge William Ambler (owner of the real estate company that brought the litigation), Robert H. Whitten (the noted city planner who at the time was based in Cleveland), Judge D. C. Westenhaver (the federal trial court judge in the case), and others. Their stories and their interrelationships add significant layers of meaning and interest to the *Euclid v. Ambler* tale.

The Village of Euclid's first zoning law, Ordinance No. 2812, was passed by a unanimous vote of the village council on November 13, 1922, only nineteen years after Euclid was incorporated and thus severed from the more expansive, original Euclid tract. At the beginning of 1922, Brigadier General Charles X. Zimmerman, who had moved to the village only a couple of years before, began his service as mayor. A veteran of the Spanish-American War who served in France during the World War I, Mayor Zimmerman appointed a four-member planning commission: James Metzenbaum (the only lawyer), Ralph L. Fuller, Paul E. Kroehle, and Harry Petee. The commission was charged with drafting a zoning ordinance that followed the guidelines established in Ohio's new enabling legislation, which went into effect on May 13, 1920. The Ohio law predated and exerted a strong influence on the State Zoning Enabling Act (SZEA), which was promulgated and popularized by the U.S. Department of Commerce in the mid-1920s.

The key appointee to the planning commission was Metzenbaum, who served as the village's zealous counsel in the eventual litigation. This lawyer, Cleveland born, raised, and educated (at Western Reserve University law school), had once resided in the village for over a decade "in a big house on Euclid Avenue" with his wife, the former Bessie Brenner, until her untimely death in 1920. After her death, Metzenbaum shuttered their Euclid home and moved into Cleveland's Statler Hotel. According to Zimmerman and Metzenbaum, the commission took very seriously its charge of protecting the health, safety, and welfare of the community, while taking care not to work hardships on landowners. Metzenbaum's testimony submitted to the trial court revealed that, from May to November 1922, the commission held regular meetings in the evening, roughly twice a week. The discussions often ran to midnight and even beyond. The commission solicited expert advice from the village engineer and from counterparts in other municipalities in the Cleveland region, gathered opinions on the zoning ordinance and map from property owners and other residents of the village, and reviewed New York's landmark ordinance and those of other major cities.

According to Mayor Zimmerman's testimony submitted to the trial court, the drafters of Euclid's ordinance "secured the primer that is issued by Mr. Hoover's department at Washington, and we gave this matter careful and faithful thought for months, in order to accomplish what we thought was for the benefit of Euclid Village, from a sanitation, from a health, from a police, and from a welfare point of view." Almost certainly, the mayor was referring to the Commerce Department's release of the September 15, 1922, version of the SZEA.

The six-month investigatory process culminated in a public hearing on November 13, 1922, following the state statute–mandated thirty days' notice. In his testimony for the trial court, prepared thirteen months later, Mayor Zimmerman recalled the meeting:

The town hall was virtually filled with people and all of the councilmen were present. . . . There was no so called protest made there to this ordinance on the part of those who resided in the Village of Euclid. There were two questions asked, if I remember rightly, in reference to the Zoning Ordinance, by residents of the Village. A great many of the property owners, and representatives of such property owners that live outside of the Village, were present, especially those that were interested in the so called industrial section of the Village. . . . That particular public hearing lasted probably three and one half hours.

The council's minutes for the November 13 meeting reported the 6–0 vote in favor of the ordinance introduced by Mr. Cantlon, "establishing a zoning plan, regulating the location of industries, trades, apartment houses, two family houses, single family houses and other uses of property, the area and dimensions of lots and yards, the bulk and alignment of buildings near street frontages." The minutes list the names of no fewer than seventeen witnesses who spoke on the motion, including representatives of the Cleveland Tractor Company, the Nickel Plate Road, the S. H. Kleinman Realty Company, and the Ajax Mfg. Company.

One of those present at the public hearing who spoke before the vote was taken to adopt Ordinance 2812 was William Ambler, the secretary and treasurer of the Ambler Realty Company, which would become the corporate plaintiff in the federal lawsuit that aimed to invalidate the ordinance. This William Ambler was the son of the company president, Judge William E. Ambler; Judge Ambler had a long record of developing real estate in the Cleveland metropolitan area. A biographical entry published in 1918 reported that Judge Ambler, who was born in Medina, Ohio, practiced law for many years in Michigan, the state to which his family had moved when he was fourteen. He had a distinguished career in Michigan as a lawyer, state senator (two terms including service as president pro tem), and probate judge, and he served as the chair of Hillsdale College's board of trustees. In 1919, Judge Ambler donated to Hillsdale, his alma mater, a building that is now called Ambler House. By that time, Judge Ambler had long been pursuing his second career—real estate development.

Judge Ambler, whose role in the development of Ambler Heights was discussed in Chapter 2, returned to his native Ohio in 1891 and was active in real estate companies and a building and loan until his death in 1925, at which time his company's suit challenging Euclid's zoning ordinance was pending before the U.S. Supreme Court. The judge's son, also named William, joined the real estate business after a short university teaching career. In his testimony at the trial court level, William the younger described a shift in the operations of the family business from "what would be called a regular [residential] subdividing business" to "the purchase of industrial sites" as well as "the purchase and sale . . . of apartment houses, terraces, single and two-family residences." In 1911, the Ambler Realty Company purchased undeveloped land located between the Nickel Plate Road and Euclid Avenue and adjoining a subdivision developed by Judge Ambler. When lots in the neighboring subdivision were sold by the family business, they were bound by private residential restrictions. By late 1922, Ambler Realty owned a parcel in this area that covered a fraction over 68 acres.

The judge's son had a much different perspective on the public hearing than the mayor:

> Various property owners were heard there in opposition to the Ordinance and there was an hour or so spent in discussion. At the time of that hearing the council passed the Ordinance. There was somebody representing the Ambler Realty Company at that hearing. They strenuously opposed the Ordinance as did all the others that were there, and there were representatives there of most of this vacant acreage between Euclid Avenue and the Nickel Plate track.

As indicated by both accounts of the council meeting, the major bone of contention at the public hearing concerned the availability of village land for industrial purposes, particularly those lands lying between Euclid Avenue—one of the three main east-west thorough-fares running between Cleveland and the Village of Euclid (the other two were Lake Shore Boulevard and St. Clair Avenue)—and the Nickel Plate Road, whose main line linked Cleveland with Chicago and Buffalo, New York.

The result of the village's investigatory and legislative efforts was a comprehensive zoning ordinance featuring a preamble and thirty substantive sections. Anyone familiar with New York's ordinance or the provisions of the proposed SZEA would not have been surprised at Euclid's work product. The "Whereas" paragraphs that prefaced the ordinance revealed several key elements that would emerge in the subsequent court proceedings. For example, the drafters referred to Euclid as a "residential suburb" of Cleveland. Both words were revealing, the first because it described the predominant use of land in the village, the second because it acknowledged a geographic tie to the central city. In further support of the initial point, the preamble noted that "a considerable part of the property [in the village] has been restricted for private residence by the owners thereof and much of the restricted property has been further limited to single residences." In other words, there would be nothing radical about superimposing public restrictions on existing private controls such as covenants.

The preamble also declared that the village's sewer and water systems were inadequate to support "more congested use," that the amount of land that the ordinance "made available for manufacturing, industrial and commercial uses is . . . sufficient for such purposes," and that the village's citizens desired "to preserve the present character of said Village and the public improvements therein, to prevent congestion, and to promote and provide for the health, safety, convenience, comfort, prosperity, and general welfare of the citizens thereof." All of these assertions reflected the concerns and aspirations of the typical suburban zoning ordinance not only in the 1920s but through the early twenty-first century as well.

In addition, the substantive provisions of the ordinance were not unusual by either contemporary or current standards. The ordinance divided the village into "six classes of use districts termed respectively class U1 or single family house districts, class U2 or two family house districts, class U3 or apartment house districts, class U4 or local retail and wholesale store districts, class U5 or commercial districts and class U6 or industrial and manufacturing districts." There were as well "three classes of height districts" (H1, H2, and H3) and "four classes of area districts" (A1, A2, A3, and A4). A zoning map indicating the location of each district was made an official part of the zoning ordinance. The ordinance mandated compliance with the ordinance, specifying, "No buildings or premises shall be erected or used except in conformity with the regulations herein prescribed for the respective use, height and area district in which such building or premises are located." By virtue of the zoning ordinance, each parcel of land in the town would have three new legal restrictions regarding the permitted use, height, and area occupied by structures on the land.

Following a definitional section that included twenty-two entries, the ordinance listed the specific uses that would be permitted in the six classes of use districts, ranging from the most restrictive (U1) to the most inclusive (U6). While U1 was described as "Single-family House," also permitted as uses in these districts would be public parks, water towers, reservoirs, electric railway passenger stations and rights of way (but not railway yards), and farming and other agricultural pursuits. At the other end of the spectrum, landowners in the U6 "Industrial" districts would be allowed to operate, among other businesses, sewage disposal plants and gas producing plants, garbage or refuse incineration, and scrap iron or junk storage. The ordinance also included a list of prohibited uses referred to as U7, even though there would be no district for these forbidden uses designated on the zoning map. Deemed out of bounds for health and safety of the village were, among others, such uses as veterinary hospitals, manufacture or storage of explosives and fireworks, cement or chlorine manufacture, ore smelting, stockyards, slaughterhouses, tanneries, and oil refineries.

Zoning in Euclid was cumulative, as was zoning in New York City and generally in other municipalities for the first few decades of its existence. This meant, for example, that landowners in the U4 districts ("Local Retail or Wholesale") could, if they so desired, use their properties for the purposes permitted in residential districts U1 through U3; or that, in addition to the uses listed for U6 districts, landowners there could utilize their properties for uses permitted in districts U1 through U5; and so on. In other words, under Euclid's zoning scheme, there was no such thing as a district that was exclusively commercial or industrial.

Euclid's first zoning ordinance, like today's typical counterpart, permitted certain "accessory uses" that were "customarily incident" to the residences permitted in the U1 through U3 districts such as private garages and certain home occupations such as medical or dental practices. The ordinance did not permit signs and billboards as accessory uses, however, with the exception of "for rent" or "for sale" signs. There were separate accessory use provisions for nonresidential districts.

There were additional provisions providing flexibility for landowners who felt unduly restricted by use districting. In certain circumstances, the City Planning and Zoning Commission was authorized to grant permission for building extensions and exceptions. Other landowners, at the time the ordinance became law, were already using their properties for purposes inconsistent with the uses that were then designated for their districts. These owners were allowed to continue, but not to substantially expand, their "non-conforming uses." This was an important way to insure against claims that zoning took away vested and existing, as opposed to anticipated, private property rights.

The ordinance described height restrictions by feet or stories; for example, structures in H2 districts could not exceed four stories or 50 feet, subject to exceptions for structures such as church spires and clock towers. Lot area limitations were expressed in terms of square footage per family; for example, dwellings or apartment houses in A3 districts could not accommodate more than one family per 1,250 feet of the area of an interior lot, or 1,000 feet of the area of a corner lot. There were separate provisions mandating side and rear yards for buildings in residence and business districts. These provisions could be quite detailed. In U1 and U2 districts, for example, "along the side line of a corner lot, the distance of the building line back from the street line shall be 15 per cent of the average width of such lot, but such distance back from the street line need not be more than 15 feet." Responsibility for the enforcement of this and other building restrictions was assigned to the inspector of buildings, in compliance with the rules and regulations of the Board of Zoning Appeals.

The board would hold public meetings and record member votes to consider issues such as appeals brought by landowners "claiming to be adversely affected by [the inspector's] decision." One provision provided an important avenue of relief for landowners who felt mistreated by the zoning scheme as applied specifically to their properties: "Where there are practical difficulties or unnecessary hardships in the way of carrying out of the strict letter of the provisions of this

Ordinance, [the board] shall have power, in a specific case, to interpret any such provision in harmony with the general purpose and intent of the Ordinance, so that the public health, safety and general welfare may be secured and so that substantial justice may be done." Although the specific term was not used, the quoted provision described the standard for granting a "variance" from the restrictions imposed by the ordinance in certain circumstances. Thus, like the provision on nonconforming uses and a separate provision allowing buildings under construction to be completed under preordinance rules, the variance provision provided additional protection against claims that zoning was an attack on constitutionally protected property rights.

Unlike ancient hieroglyphics, the zoning map would not be carved in stone. The village council was specifically authorized "from time to time, on its own motion or on petition, after public notice and hearing, [to] amend the regulations and districts" set by the original ordinance. Such proposed changes would first be submitted to the City Planning and Zoning Commission for review, and a negative report from the commission could only be overridden by a three-fourths majority of the council.

Each violation of the ordinance could result in a misdemeanor conviction, with a maximum fine of $500, to be multiplied by the total number of days during which the offense continued. As the drafters believed uses of the property inconsistent with the ordinance were "imminent and that such uses would permanently injure or partially nullify such orderly plan of development, and injure such necessary public health, safety and general welfare," the emergency ordinance went into immediate effect on its date of passage.

This regulatory creature—comprehensive height, area, and use zoning—did not even exist a decade before Euclid's version was enacted. By November 13, 1922, the village was joining hundreds of American communities that had taken an important and dramatic step toward segregating seemingly incompatible uses of land by flexing their police power muscles in a manner that was bound to attract a legal response from disgruntled landowners.

Within a few days after the passage of its first zoning ordinance, the village, like many other local governments that adopted this new form of land regulation, was sued in the state court of common pleas.

Metzenbaum, who had just been named the first chair of the Zoning Board of Appeals, was charged with defending the new ordinance in a state trial court, apparently without compensation. In his 1930 work, *The Law of Zoning*, Metzenbaum wrote that, "in an effort to set forth a full and comprehensive presentation of the philosophy and of the principles of zoning, the writer made an effort to collate every then known decision which had been rendered upon the subject." The village won the case, titled *State* ex rel. *Cormiea v. Stein*, and distributed the results of Metzenbaum's research widely to assist the many other local governments facing landowner challenges to zoning. This research task would prepare Metzenbaum well for a more momentous case that would soon arise.

The November 13 meeting was not the last time that village officials would address the concerns of Ambler Realty and the other owners in the "industrial section." The topic of expanding the industrial zone in the vicinity of Ambler's 68-acre tract was the subject of several subsequent meetings of village zoning and planning officials, with representatives of industrial interests including Ambler Realty present, that took place after Mayor Zimmerman returned to Euclid from a European trip in February 1923. In his trial court testimony, Zimmerman recalled that those seeking a change had conceded that "the proposition [of the original zoning ordinance] was all right, it was simply that it reduced the value of their particular piece of land." In the meantime, the "industrialists" also apparently met several times on their own at the Athletic Club to discuss the issue of zoning.

Opponents of Euclid's zoning ordinance also reached out to one of the most important legal and political figures in Cleveland, indeed the nation, in early 1923. On March 16, 1923, Newton Diehl Baker, a founder of the Cleveland law firm of Baker, Hostetler & Sidlo, wrote the following in a letter to William Ambler of the Ambler Realty Company:

Mr. Morgan [Robert M. Morgan, from the Cleveland firm of Fackler & Morgan] and I have conferred about the litigation to test the Euclid zoning ordinance, and are well advanced with the preliminary inquiries which are necessary to be made before the suit is instituted. It is our present purpose to file the action in the

United States District Court here in Cleveland, and if necessary, to take it from there to the Supreme Court of the United States directly if possible.

You and your associates were desirous of knowing what the probable expenses of the litigation would be. We are agreed that the attorneys' fees shall not exceed $10,000. . . . It is difficult to forecast with certainty the probable amount of such costs [making maps, printing briefs, court fees, and the like], but we think they would not exceed $1,000 in any case.

This would not be an inexpensive proposition, but Baker was already anticipating that the case might reach the nation's highest tribunal. In April, Ambler Realty was one of fifteen large landowners in the village to execute an "expense underwriting agreement" to cover legal fees and other expenses to be incurred by Baker and his legal team.

In 1923, Newton D. Baker was a household name not only in Cleveland and Ohio, but throughout the nation and abroad as well. A native of Martinsburg, West Virginia, Baker graduated from Johns Hopkins University in 1892, where he got to know Woodrow Wilson, who at the time was a visiting lecturer from Princeton University. Baker received his law degree two years later from Washington & Lee University and returned to Martinsburg to practice law for a short while, until he moved to Washington, D.C., to serve as the private secretary to the postmaster general in the second administration of Democratic president Grover Cleveland. When that post ended upon William McKinley's inauguration as president, Baker returned to Martinsburg and formed the law partnership of Flick, Westenhaver & Baker. David C. (D. C.) Westenhaver, like Baker a native West Virginian, became president of the state bar association in 1898.

The following year, Baker moved to Cleveland to practice law. At first Baker lived with an old Johns Hopkins friend, Frederic C. Howe. In 1901, Baker began twenty years of nearly uninterrupted public service when he became legal adviser to Cleveland's Board of Equalization. He soon became the city's law director, and when in 1903 that position became an elected post with the title of solicitor, Baker was the first occupant. The mayor from 1901 to 1909 was Tom L. Johnson — Democrat, street railway line owner-turned-Progressive reformer, and a strong believer in Henry George's idea that government should be financed by a "single tax" on the unimproved value of land. Baker and Howe were two of Johnson's young allies, and as city solicitor, Baker proved to be one of the mayor's most effective workers and closest friends. He was a major participant in the struggle to establish a three-cent fare on the city's street railways. The ultimate failure of that effort spelled doom for Johnson's reelection effort in 1909. Two years later, Johnson was dead, so, beginning in 1912, Baker picked up his mentor's mantle by serving two mayoral terms.

As mayor, Baker was a strong and successful advocate for home rule, a legal change that would make municipalities more autonomous and less subject to control by the state legislature. That legal change was accomplished by an amendment to the Ohio Constitution in 1912, which meant that, upon his reelection, Baker would be Cleveland's first home rule mayor. He believed in municipal ownership of public utilities, prompting his opponents to label Baker a radical. He worked hard to revitalize downtown Cleveland with a new City Hall next door to a new Union Station.

In 1912, Baker cast his lot with Progressive Democrat Woodrow Wilson and achieved national notoriety for his impassioned oratory at the party's convention that year in Baltimore. When his second mayoral term ended in 1916, Baker returned to private practice, forming the new firm of Baker, Hostetler & Sidlo, but the resignation of Secretary of War Lindley M. Garrison on February 10 led to an offer that Baker could not refuse. At forty-four, Baker would be the youngest member of the Wilson cabinet, at a time when Europe was engulfed in world war. Five months after Wilson was reelected in part because "he kept us out of war," the United States was embroiled in the conflict. Baker, who was a committed pacifist, faced major challenges involving issues such as the draft, the care and training for millions of soldiers in uniform, the status of conscientious objectors, the review of death penalties in courts-martial, and the coordination of American military leadership with the allies. Baker returned to the law firm that he founded in the spring of 1921, and only two years later he would find himself involved in the fight to invalidate zoning in Euclid, and perhaps, beyond.

Thanks to a member of Baker's firm who decades later provided details from Baker's case file, we can read the text of the subscription to which the New York Central and Nickel Plate rail lines contributed $2,000 each, in which the subscribers were described as landowners in the village who "believe their rights as such owners are seriously prejudiced by the provisions" of Ordinance 2812. One other "Whereas" paragraph explained that these landowners were opening their checkbooks for the purpose "of having an appropriate action or actions . . . to test the validity of said Ordinance in such court or courts as counsel selected may in his or their discretion think best." The document, which designated Baker "as attorney and counsel in such matters," delegated to him "the right in his discretion to select other attorneys as he wishes to aid him in the matter, at his own expense." On May 5, 1923, even before the meetings in Euclid designed to produce industrial landowner–friendly amendments were concluded, Baker acted on behalf of his named client—Ambler Realty Company—by filing a complaint in the District Court of the United States for the District of Ohio against the Village of Euclid and Harry W. Stein, the village's inspector of buildings. There were actually three cases—one brought by Ambler Realty Company, the others brought by individual owners of two other parcels in the village (W. E. Ambler and Fisher). By all accounts, this would be the first federal court challenge to comprehensive zoning, and it was destined to be the most significant and memorable.

In contrast to the untraveled litigation route that Ambler Realty was pursuing, by 1923 several similarly situated landowners had already filed suit in various state courts seeking to invalidate zoning ordinances in whole or in part. It would be an extreme understatement to say that the state of the decisional law on zoning in the early 1920s was in flux. Confused would be a more accurate description. In some instances, state courts found that in the absence of a state statute authorizing the use of the zoning device individual municipalities did not have the inherent power to create zoning districts. This was the holding in 1920 by the Michigan Supreme Court in *Clements v. McCabe*, a case in which Detroit, a city with home rule powers, hastily drew up an ordinance creating residential zones in response to efforts by a landowner to build an "automobile battery service station." The court reasoned:

The controlling test is whether by any adequate, definite provision in the Constitution or general act passed pursuant to it cities have been vested with this evolutionary and comprehensive police power of zoning asserted here. Independent of legislation, the Constitution confers no such grant of power directly upon cities. Assuming, but not deciding, that such power is by the Constitution committed to the legislature, it has not by express grant in adequate terms delegated the same to cities.

Notice that the court was assuming, but not yet deciding, the constitutional question of whether even the *state* had the power to authorize zoning.

That same year, the Supreme Judicial Court of Massachusetts informed the state legislature in an advisory opinion (In re *Opinion of the Justices* [1920]) that a proposed statute authorizing a form of zoning would not be unconstitutional. The proposed bill would authorize municipalities to "restrict buildings to be used for particular industries, trades, manufacturing or commercial purposes to specified parts of the city or town, or may exclude them from specified parts of the city or town, or may provide that such buildings, if situated in certain parts of the city or town, shall be subject to special regulations as to their construction or use." The highest tribunal in Massachusetts found that the proposed scheme did not go beyond constitutional bounds, despite the fact that the legislation had an aesthetic flavor, as long as urban design was not the sole purpose of the legislation:

Enhancement of the artistic attractiveness of the city or town can be considered in exercising the power conferred by the proposed act only when the dominant aim in respect to the establishment of districts based on use and construction of buildings has primary regard to other factors lawfully within the scope of the police power; and then it can be considered, not as the main purpose to be attained, but only as subservient to another or other main ends recognized as sufficient under [Massachusetts constitutional] Amendment 60 and the general principles governing the exercise of the police power.

As the 1920s progressed, some state courts would follow Massachusetts's lead, while others, like Michigan's high court, would declare zoning invalid, either because zoning was not specifically permitted by state statute or because as applied to the claims of a specific landowner it proved to be unreasonable or confiscatory.

Before and soon after Ambler Realty and its allies in the industrial community decided to pursue a federal court strategy, other disgruntled Ohio landowners had decided to take their chances in state court. The experience in Ohio's state courts is particularly instructive and relevant, first, because the judges were interpreting local ordinances based on the same principles of state decisional, statutory, and constitutional law, and second, because state law during this short time period underwent a subtle though significant shift in favor of the constitutional validity of zoning.

Even before New York–style zoning reached the Buckeye State, Ohio courts had given their approval to incremental building regulations. For example, in 1918, the Supreme Court of Ohio upheld a provision in Cleveland's building code that required tenement houses more than 35 feet or three stories in height to use fireproof construction. In *State* ex rel. *Euclid-Doan Building Co. v. Cunningham* (1918), the court applied the provision to the owner of a five-story building on Euclid Avenue who wanted to convert the top floor to apartments for eleven families. The supreme court affirmed the trial court's refusal to issue a building permit in the absence of the owner's compliance with safety requirements. The same year, in *State* ex rel. *Ohio Hair Products Co. v. Rendigs*, the state supreme court refused to order the city of Cincinnati to reissue a building permit to a landowner who proposed to enter into the business "of buying, selling, processing and manufacturing the hair of animals and packing-house by-products." The business owner was originally granted a construction permit, but owing to the subsequent enactment of an ordinance banning such businesses from residential areas of the city, the permit was revoked. The supreme court rejected the company's constitutional claims, again relying on the city's traditional police power:

In the instant case, the determination of the question whether or not the ordinance was reasonably necessary for the protection of the health and comfort of those within the locality in question was committed in the first instance to the judgment of the municipal authority. If, in the exercise of the discretion conferred upon it, the municipality acted reasonably, and not arbitrarily, its action is not subject to objection and will not be disturbed.

Even though the business would not necessarily be a nuisance, it could be excluded from certain neighborhoods by government regulation.

When localities began to implement true zoning ordinances, the state courts sent inconsistent messages. Two of the early cases came from Cleveland suburbs that relied on Robert Whitten's drafting expertise. In *State* ex rel. *Morris v. East Cleveland* (1919), six days before the city passed its zoning ordinance, and one year before the state zoning enabling act went into effect, Max Morris applied to the building inspector for permits to allow construction of apartment houses on his parcels. Because the new ordinance did not allow apartments in the districts in which Morris's parcels were located, he was refused permission to build. Morris claimed that the purpose of the zoning ordinance was to prevent his construction plans. While the landowner claimed that the issue was whether the ordinance was unconstitutional because "it, in effect, takes property without due process of law," the trial court begged to differ: "The proposition before the court is simply this: Had the municipality of East Cleveland a right to pass the zone building ordinance, in the exercise of its police power?" Instead of focusing solely on the rights of the developer, the court asked, "We will suppose, for instance, that a street in East Cleveland has fifty or a hundred beautiful residences, with well-kept lawns and shade trees, free from the contaminating effects of the odors and smoke of factories, and the incessant, discordant noises, smoke and other evils of apartment houses, can it be said that the owners of these dwellings, and the inhabitants of this street, have no rights which others are bound to respect?" While apartment houses might be needed in cities such as London, New York, Paris, "it is not true in a city like Cleveland, or East Cleveland, where the whole county is available for residence purposes."

After engaging in a rambling discourse about the evils of apartment houses, the rapaciousness of landlords, and the health dangers posed by overpopulation, the court noted that this form of development threatened the well-being of the region: "The number of apartment houses, terraces and tenement blocks in Cleveland, Lakewood and East Cleveland, and the rapidity with which their construction is increasing, is appalling. They may be numbered by the thousand." In the end, it came down to the question of who carried the burden—was it the responsibility of the city to show that its newfangled ordinance was reasonable, or did the landowner have to show that the duly enacted measure lacked rationality? The judge cast his lot in favor of the municipality: "the burden is upon the relator [Morris] to show that the ordinance is unreasonable, clearly so, and that the means adopted in the ordinance are not suitable to the end in view, and that the ordinance is not impartial in operation, and is unduly oppressive upon individuals, and has not a real and substantial relation to the purposes and ends in view." Proving a negative was and remains a very heavy chore indeed. The court, therefore, refused to grant Morris's wish for an immediate order, but remained open to a rehearing at which all of the facts and evidence could be put forward. When that rehearing occurred, another trial judge again sided with the city, finding that the ordinance was "a valid exercise of the police power" and "that it has not been shown that the classifications made under this ordinance are unreasonable, arbitrary, discriminatory and not uniform in operation."

Four years after the *Morris* case, the question of the validity of another Whitten-assisted zoning ordinance was presented to a state appeals court. In *State v. Durant*, Lakewood's building inspector refused to issue a building permit to allow the construction of a three-story brick apartment house, as the use would not be in compliance with the city's zoning ordinance. The trial court refused to order the inspector to grant the permit, despite the landowner's constitutional claims. Even though the appeals court "conceded that the weight of authority in the United States is against its [a general zoning ordinance's] constitutionality," the lower court decision in favor of Lakewood was affirmed on the basis of Ohio statutory and constitutional law, including the new Ohio zoning enabling act. This decision, handed down a few months after Ambler Realty's decision to file its lawsuit against Euclid, sent a mixed message to Baker. On the one hand, the court acknowledged that other courts had decided against zoning; on the other hand, this Ohio landowner lost.

Under the rules prevailing at the time Baker filed the lawsuit, one of the ways for a plaintiff to get into (and stay in) federal court, was to demonstrate that it had suffered an economic loss of at least $3,000 and that the claim was one, in the words of Article III of the Constitution, "arising under this Constitution, the Laws of the United States, and Treaties." Ambler Realty alleged both, claiming more specifically that its action was "brought to redress the deprivation of the plaintiff of its property without due process of law under color of the laws and statutes of the state of Ohio . . . and to secure the plaintiff the equal protection of the law which is guaranteed to it by the constitution of the United States and of the State of Ohio and of which it is threatened to be deprived by the action of the State of Ohio." A large part of the complaint provided details on the geography of Euclid and its location in the path of metropolitan Cleveland's industrial expansion. The focus of the complaint then narrowed to Euclid's 68-acre parcel, with a full-blown legal description. Baker and his cocounsel Morgan then provided a detailed summary of Ordinance 2812 (the full text was included as an appendix) and averred that the effect of the ordinance on their client was to "so limit, restrict and control the lawful use of its said lands as to confiscate and destroy a great part of the value thereof." Moreover, Ambler Realty's counsel alleged "that prospective buyers of land for industrial, commercial and residential uses in the metropolitan district of Cleveland are deterred from buying any part of the lands of this plaintiff by the existence of said ordinance, being unwilling to consider land as to which it will be necessary for them to conduct burdensome and expensive litigation in order to vindicate their right to subject it to lawful and legitimate uses." Ambler Realty also claimed that the ordinance "was enacted for the purpose of preserving the ideas of beauty officially entertained by the members of the [village] council." For these and other reasons, the ordinance allegedly violated Ambler Realty's protections under the due process and equal protection clauses of the Fourteenth Amendment of the U.S. Constitution, and under similar and related provisions in the Ohio Constitution.

Although Ambler Realty claimed that it had already suffered an economic loss upon the enactment of Ordinance 2812, the plaintiff was not seeking monetary damages for the alleged violations of constitutional protections. The plaintiff instead asked the court to "hold and declare said ordinance No. 2812 to be illegal and void" and to grant a "writ of injunction commanding" the village and its officials "to absolutely desist and refrain from any attempted enforcement of the provisions" of the ordinance. Because the landowner was seeking this kind of "injunctive" remedy, as opposed to seeking a monetary award, the judge would try the case without using a jury.

The village's next important legal maneuver would not occur in the federal court. On June 11, 1923, in accordance with the provisions allowing changes in the original ordinance, the Council of Euclid Village, upon the recommendation of the Planning and Zoning Commission, adopted Ordinances 3366, 3367, and 3368, amending the original zoning scheme. Ordinance 3366 expanded the list of uses permitted in U3 districts to include office buildings and other non-residential uses. The second and third measures were directly responsive to the concerns of Judge Ambler and the other speculators in industrial land. Ordinance 3367 expanded the U6 "industrial and manufacturing" district that was located south of Nickel Plate tracks (this included Ambler Realty's 68-acre parcel). The final change, effected by Ordinance 3368, inserted a new U3 district south of the newly expanded U6 district. The immediate effect on Ambler Realty's 68-acre parcel was to reduce the portion of the parcel (adjoining Euclid Avenue) that was originally zoned U2. In its place, a strip of land north of what remained in the U2 district was placed in a U3 district, and the remainder of the parcel (extending north to the tracks) was zoned U6. The result was that the first 630 feet from Euclid Avenue were zoned U2, the next 130 feet were zoned U3, and the remaining roughly 1,000 feet were zoned U6.

If village officials thought that Ambler's lawsuit would fade away in the light of these concessions, they were sadly mistaken. Good citizen Metzenbaum—of the Cleveland firm of Metzenbaum, Lurie, Addams & Burke—was again called upon to handle the defense of the (now amended) ordinance, though for a much more modest legal fee than his very formidable chief opponent. News that the case was assigned to Judge D. C. Westenhaver would not have been heartening to Metzenbaum and his clients.

Westenhaver had been Baker's mentor and law partner when both men lived in Martinsburg, West Virginia. Baker moved to Cleveland in 1899 and immediately became immersed in single-taxer Tom L. Johnson's reform struggles. Westenhaver, a Georgetown-educated lawyer who had served as a local prosecutor and city council member in Martinsburg, joined his former law partner in Cleveland in 1903, and the two teamed up in battles over street railway franchises. Some of the cases in which Baker and Westenhaver joined forces were carried all the way to the U.S. Supreme Court. For example, in 1904 and 1906 decisions carrying the same name — *Cleveland v. Cleveland Electric Railway Company* — Baker and Westenhaver represented the city, unsuccessfully as it turned out, in fare and contract disputes with one franchisee. In 1907, City Solicitor Baker represented Cleveland, and Westenhaver, his former law partner, argued on behalf of the Forest City Railway in a more successful effort against Cleveland Electric, which was represented by lawyers from Squire, Sanders & Dempsey, another preeminent Cleveland law firm then and today.

In 1916, when Justice Charles Evans Hughes resigned his seat on the High Court in order to run on the Republican ticket against President Wilson, Baker had used his considerable influence to help secure a U.S. Supreme Court seat for another close friend, Ohio federal district judge John H. Clarke. Opposing Baker in his lobbying effort were supporters of defeated president William Howard Taft (a sentimental favorite) and of George Sutherland, the former U.S. Senator from Utah (championed by Ohio Senator Warren G. Harding). Clarke would hold the post until he resigned in 1922 to campaign for U.S. membership in the League of Nations, an effort that proved to be futile. At that point, then-president Harding would use this opportunity to get Sutherland onto the Court.

In 1916, Westenhaver was named to Clarke's former position in the U.S. District Court for the Northern District of Ohio, a move about which the *Cleveland Plain Dealer* proclaimed: "Westenhaver, Baker's Choice, Named U.S. District Judge." Two years later, national attention was focused on Westenhaver's courtroom, when he sentenced Eugene V. Debs, the labor leader and five-time Socialist Party presidential candidate, to a ten-year prison sentence for violating the Espionage Act of 1917. The events leading to Debs's arrest were later summarized by Justice Holmes, in his opinion for a unanimous Supreme Court in *Debs v. United States* (1919), affirming the conviction:

On or about June 16, 1918, at Canton, Ohio, the defendant caused and incited and attempted to cause and incite insubordination, disloyalty, mutiny and refusal of duty in the military and naval forces of the United States and with intent so to do delivered, to an assembly of people, a public speech, set forth. The fourth count alleges that he obstructed and attempted to obstruct the recruiting and enlistment service of the United States and to that end and with that intent delivered the same speech, again set forth.

One of the Department of Justice attorneys assisting in the case before the High Court was a prominent Cincinnati lawyer named Alfred Bettman. A few weeks after Debs began serving his sentence, Cleveland erupted in violent May Day riots.

Like Westenhaver, Metzenbaum was aligned politically with Baker. According to a remembrance of Euclid's attorney published shortly after his death, Baker (in 1913) had recommended Metzenbaum to head Cleveland's Young Democrats. By the early 1920s, Metzenbaum would be aware not only of Baker's ample skills as a lawyer and politician, but also of the close connection between his opponent and the judge who would hear the zoning case. The defendants' first move in court, on July 20, 1923, was to file a motion to dismiss Ambler Realty's bill of complaint. In this short document, Metzenbaum merely claimed that the facts stated by the plaintiff did not entitle it to relief and did not state a cause of action, and, presumably because of the June amendments, the complaint "presents nothing more than a moot question." Almost four months later, on November 9, Judge Westenhaver entertained arguments on Metzenbaum's motion, which he then overruled "after due consideration." On November 12, Baker reported to one of his clients that only the Ambler Realty case would proceed. Once "the constitutional question has been disposed of in the Ambler Realty Company case," then a similar order would be entered for the other two cases (brought by W. E. Ambler and Fisher).

Now that the case was proceeding toward a substantive resolution, Metzenbaum filed his answer, most of which was the typical point-by-point denial found in standard answers in civil lawsuits. Some of the major points that Metzenbaum sought to clarify for the court were that Euclid had experienced rapid growth in population recently; that there was a small number of factories then located in the village (sixteen total and only two on Euclid Avenue); that, far from suffering a loss, Ambler Realty "will actually benefit, financially and otherwise, by virtue of these [zoning] restrictions"; that the June 11 amendments (appended to the answer) permitted the plaintiff to "use all of his [sic] land which may reasonably be used for industrial or factory purposes"; that the zoning ordinance was not "enacted for the mere purpose of preserving the idea of beauty or for mere aesthetic purposes"; and that the village "has had a decided and, at times, critical insufficiency of water" for more than five years. There were indubitably serious gaps between the versions of reality conveyed by the competing parties in the initial written arguments that they submitted to the court.

The testimony in the case did not take place in court before Judge Westenhaver. Instead, in accordance with an agreement between the parties, the lawyers conducted depositions in Cleveland between December 18 and 29, 1923. Fourteen witnesses were called in this relatively brief period, some more than once. The testimony, which often included cross-examination and even re-cross-examination, focused on four main issues: (1) the value of the 68-acre parcel before and after passage of the zoning ordinance, (2) the process that led to the passage of the ordinance and the amendments, (3) the residential and industrial real estate market in metropolitan Cleveland and in and near the Village of Euclid, and (4) the adequacy of the water supply that Cleveland provided to the village. In addition to oral testimony, aerial and earth-bound photographs were discussed, lending a modern flavor to the proceedings. Among the parties whose testimony was recorded and submitted to the court were Mayor Zimmerman, William Ambler (the younger), James Metzenbaum, Harry W. Stein, and Robert Whitten.

Ambler's assertion that the 68-acre parcel was worth $10,000 an acre unrestricted and $2,000 if limited to residential use was hotly contested by opposing counsel and the witnesses for the village. Ambler also offered these observations regarding the potential for high-end residential development in Euclid:

> Considering Cleveland and its suburbs, the high class residence territory in the Cleveland district is that section known as the Heights, embraced largely by Shaker Heights and Cleveland Heights, together with the Wade Park district, including the Lake

Shore frontage in limited amounts. There is a very large amount of residence property available for development in Cleveland Heights and Shaker Heights. I don't believe this territory in Euclid Village, south of Euclid Avenue and overlooking the Nickel Plate and the New York Central tracks, could be sold as high class residence property.

Witnesses for the village were more sanguine about future residential development patterns, and former Ohio Lieutenant Governor William A. Greenlund, drawing on his real estate experience, opined: "I have no hesitancy in saying that there is a surplus of industrial property at the present time, available in and around the city of Cleveland and along the various railroads entering in Cleveland. . . . I don't know of any demand for industrial property in the Village of Euclid today."

Given his opportunity to speak on behalf of zoning, the expert consultant Whitten observed that "zoning promotes industrial and commercial efficiency, prevents enormous waste and conserves property values." Hundreds of transcribed pages were turned over to the judge for his serious consideration.

Metzenbaum was not alone in his defense of Euclid's zoning scheme. He was joined by counsel for two *amici curiae* ("friends of the court"): the Cleveland Chamber of Commerce (represented by W. C. Boyle of Squire, Sanders & Dempsey) and the Ohio State Conference on City Planning (represented by Alfred Bettman, the nationally prominent attorney and planning advocate from Cincinnati). Unfortunately, the zealous village counsel had problems with both of these "allies." As noted in the Chapter 5, the differences between Bettman and Metzenbaum would emerge after the trial phase. The village attorney's conflict with Boyle arose earlier.

In his initial *amicus* brief, Boyle, while defending the constitutionality of the zoning ordinance as applied to the Ambler tract, conceded an important factual issue: "All unite in saying that the restriction of the first 150 feet for single- or two-family residences on Euclid Avenue is not the best or most profitable use to which it could and should be put." Metzenbaum forced Boyle to take back this concession in an amended brief, causing some embarrassment for the latter.

In a letter to "My dear Newton," mistakenly dated January 9, 1923 (not 1924), Boyle explained his predicament:

After preparing my brief . . . , I sent a copy thereof to Mr. Metzenbaum before filing it to see if it met with his approval, and upon receiving his approval I filed it. Metzenbaum had very little time to read it over, as I was very anxious to get it to the Court that evening. After a more careful perusal and study of the brief Metzenbaum objected very seriously to my conclusions and admissions therein, and wished me to withdraw the brief and make changes which would allow the Court to draw the inference of unreasonableness in the ordinance rather than to aid him in that conclusion by the admissions made. As I am not representing the Village, and he is, I felt I had no right to do any injury to his case.

Boyle then reported that Judge Westenhaver had granted him permission to withdraw and rewrite his brief.

One day later, Baker responded to "My dear Will," stating, "I perfectly understand the situation there and will, of course, seek no advantage from the frankness of our original brief, although with a judge like Westenhaver I fancy it makes very little difference whether we let him draw the inferences or aid him in drawing them." On January 11, Boyle responded in turn to Baker's understanding response: "I thank you sincerely for your very frank and manly letter of December [sic] tenth, as it greatly tends to relieve me from the embarrassment that has oppressed me throughout this trial." On the following day, Baker took an important step to neutralize any harm to the village that might have been caused by Boyle's potentially costly concession in his *amicus* brief. Baker wrote to "My dear Judge Westenhaver," requesting "that in so far as the argument in my last memorandum is based upon an admission as to the unreasonableness of the 750 foot restriction line, it be disregarded." Thus was this prominent Cleveland counsel burned by the fervent zeal of one advocate and rescued by the cool and confident graciousness of his opponent.

On January 14, 1924, Judge Westenhaver struck down the village's zoning scheme, concluding that "the ordinance involved, as applied to plaintiff's property, is unconstitutional and void; that it takes plaintiff's property, if not for private, at least for public, use, without just compensation; that it is in no just sense a reasonable or legitimate exercise of police power." Westenhaver was aware of the national debate in the early years of the twentieth century over the legitimacy and efficacy of zoning and land-use planning. He knew, too, that the case was bound for a loftier tribunal: "This case is obviously destined to go higher." The trial court judge's precognition went beyond this simple prediction, however, for contained in but one paragraph of the opinion are insights concerning the nature of twentieth-century land-use controls that would not be widely shared by other jurists for several more decades.

First, Judge Westenhaver observed that zoning artificially controls the market in land: "The plain truth is that the true object of the ordinance in question is to place all the property in an undeveloped area of 16 square miles in a strait-jacket." He then noted the discriminatory intent of Euclid's scheme: "The purpose to be accomplished is really to regulate the mode of living of persons who may hereafter inhabit it. In the last analysis, the result to be accomplished is to classify the population and segregate them according to their income or situation in life." Next, the trial judge sensed the exclusionary nature of suburban land-use patterns:

> The true reason why some persons live in a mansion and others in a shack, why some live in a single-family dwelling and others in a double-family dwelling, why some live in a two-family dwelling and others in an apartment, or why some live in a well-kept apartment and others in a tenement, is primarily economic. It is a matter of income and wealth, plus the labor and difficulty of procuring adequate domestic service.

There was a subjective, aesthetic nature to Euclid's controls as well: "Aside from contributing to these results and furthering such class tendencies, the ordinance has also an esthetic purpose; that is to say, to make this village develop into a city along lines now conceived by the village council to be attractive and beautiful." Substituting his judgment for that of local government officials, Judge Westenhaver questioned the reasonableness of the challenged regulations: "The assertion that this ordinance may tend to prevent congestion, and thereby contribute to the health and safety, would be more substantial if provision had been or could be made for adequate east and west and north and south street highways." Finally, the judge condemned the confiscation suffered by Ambler and other landowners: "Whether these purposes and objects would justify the taking of plaintiff's property as and for a public use need not be considered. It is sufficient to say that, in our opinion, and as applied to plaintiff's property, it may not be done without compensation under the guise of exercising the police power."

In their consideration of Euclid's appeal, most of the Supreme Court justices seemed to have paid little heed to the arguments and warnings provided by Judge Westenhaver, for the letter and spirit of Justice George Sutherland's opinion for the *Euclid v. Ambler* majority indicated much more respect for the village's ends and means. Over the next five decades, Westenhaver's augury would, for the most part, remain unheeded by the justices.

During that half-century, popular and expert judicial dissatisfaction with perceived irregularities and excesses by government officials has grown slowly but steadily. By the late 1980s, the jurisprudential pendulum began to swing in a counter-Euclidean direction; the result has been a collection of holdings much less favorable to land-use regulators. Today, long after its author's passing, Westenhaver's one, key paragraph could serve as a primer for law students interested in finding successful theories to be employed by property owners who choose to attack government regulation of land.

CHAPTER 5

Defending a Plan for the Village of Euclid

Euclid v. Ambler would never have became the central case in American land-use law if not for the tenacious drive of James Metzenbaum, counsel for the village. He was not about to give up when, on January 14, 1924, Judge Westenhaver rejected the arguments of Metzenbaum and the two *amici* and issued an opinion finding Euclid's ordinance null and void. In a letter to members of the Ohio Conference on City Planning, Secretary-Treasurer Charlotte Rumbold (who has been called the nation's first planning lobbyist) reported that Boyle and Bettman agreed that Westenhaver's opinion was "a barrier but not entirely an insurmountable obstacle to zoning progress in" the Buckeye State. However, the two friends of the court who supported Metzenbaum's cause were not on board with the notion of filing an appeal; instead they "hope[d] that the Euclid Village zoning authorities will amend their Ordinance in accordance with [the district court's] opinion." The following September, Bettman wrote to the city attorney of Tulsa, Oklahoma, that the village's limitation on industrial uses "was a piece of arbitrary zoning and on the facts not justifiable," and that "everybody advised against an appeal [from the District Court opinion], because on appeal the decision is sure to be affirmed, even though the upper court disagrees with the opinion."

In contrast with this hesitancy, Metzenbaum was undeterred in his crusade to vindicate zoning. He pursued an appeal to the U.S. Supreme Court, then under the leadership of fellow Ohioan William Howard Taft. Under the jurisdictional rules in place in 1924, Metzenbaum was able to go directly to the Supreme Court after the finding of one trial court judge that zoning was unconstitutional. Only one year later, the rules would change dramatically, as Congress in 1925 gave the Supreme Court more discretion in choosing the cases that it wanted to hear.

On July 10, 1925, while awaiting Metzenbaum's brief to the Supreme Court, Baker provided his clients ("Mr. Wm. Ambler and Associates") with an update of his litigation team's multifront assault on zoning. The Ambler Realty case was one of four zoning lawsuits in which Baker, Morgan, and their associates were involved: the three consolidated challenges to Euclid's Ordinance No. 2812 (which would result in the Supreme Court's holding in *Euclid v. Ambler*); a second successful federal district court case brought by Midland Bank against a Euclid nuisance ordinance; and two cases before the Supreme Court of Ohio ("Pritz" and "Kahn"), in which Baker and Morgan filed *amicus curiae* briefs challenging zoning ordinances in Cincinnati and Youngstown. Baker offered this prediction regarding the first case:

> In my opinion, if this case goes to a final hearing, the Supreme Court will write an opinion passing on the constitutional questions involved and I believe will hold that the zoning principle is in violation of the Federal Constitution. It is possible for the court to hold the particular ordinance unreasonable and therefore void, and not pass on the broad principle involved, but in view of the state of the record in that case, I do not think that will be the result. It is likely that before the case comes to a hearing, similar cases will come up from other jurisdictions, and that they will be disposed of by the court in one opinion.

As it turns out, none of Baker's predictions would be on the money.

Two years after filing the appeal, Metzenbaum submitted to the Court a brief for the appellants that, when published in book form along with the other briefs, would run for more than 140 pages. Metzenbaum would later, somewhat unbelievably, label this brief "short and concise." He spent more than 40 pages disputing Baker and Morgan's account of the facts before the trial court, nearly 30 pages defending modern zoning practice and theory, 15 pages defending zoning as a constitutional exercise of the police power, and more than 35 pages reviewing cases upholding zoning from throughout the nation.

In recounting the facts underlying the dispute, Metzenbaum attempted to refute Ambler Realty's claim that the company had suffered economic harm by the mere enactment of the ordinance. He also pointed out that, with the exception of a "small cluster of stores at the Center of the Village," the only existing buildings on that part of Euclid Avenue that ran through the municipality were residential in nature. Whereas in Cleveland the properties along Euclid Avenue were *actually* being used for business and commercial purposes, such was not the case for those properties abutting the street as it made its way eastward through the village.

In his discussion of "The Philosophy of Zoning," Metzenbaum sought to distinguish the legitimate kind of comprehensive zoning ordinance in Euclid, "a comprehensive distribution of the whole territory of the community among all the different uses, each with appropriate standards of height and occupancy," from the potentially arbitrary "block" ordinance, which "seeks to protect existing residential blocks or neighborhoods, by defining what is a residential area and prohibiting certain designated businesses or industries in that *one* block or in that one territory." It was the former regulatory device that had won judicial approval in several states, not its more problematic alternative.

Metzenbaum tried to direct the Court's attention away from the "question of the reasonableness or unreasonableness of the particular restriction" to an alternative inquiry: "the sole and completely *legal* and *fundamental* question as to whether there may be a *constitutional power* to enact such ordinances as the one in question." Metzenbaum marshaled support for a positive answer to the proper question before the Court from the "thorough investigation" preceding the adoption of New York City's 1916 ordinance, which was available to the good citizens of Euclid as they prepared their own version. The ordinance in Euclid and those adopted by municipalities throughout the nation were "substantially alike," as they were "uniformly framed after the so-called 'model' Act issued and sponsored by the Department of Commerce at Washington." Metzenbaum's vision moved beyond the United States as well, as he noted that England had made its version of districting mandatory for many of its cities.

The appellants' discussion of the police power emphasized that this important responsibility to protect the public health, safety, morals, and general welfare was reserved to the states by the Constitution. Those state and local governments that have adopted zoning statutes and ordinances "have felt that the Police Power necessarily *must keep step with* and *must keep pace with* the *new* and daily problems presented by the complexities of modern civilization, transportation and conditions." Accompanying and strengthening the police power was a judicial presumption of validity, which could be overcome only if the ordinance were "found to be clearly and plainly and manifestly unreasonable and arbitrary." This discussion led into a state-by-state review of decisions addressing the validity of zoning ordinance, including the Ohio cases culminating in *Pritz v. Messer*, in which the state supreme court had given its blessing to Cincinnati's zoning ordinance in theory. Metzenbaum closed this part of the discussion by reminding the justices of their history of deference in police power cases, quoting Justice John H. Clarke's opinion in *Thomas Cusack Co. v. City of Chicago* (1917):

> While this court has refrained from any attempt to define with precision the limits of the police power, yet its disposition is to favor the validity of laws relating to matters completely within the territory of the State enacting them and it so reluctantly disagrees with the local legislative authority, primarily the judge of the public welfare, especially when its action is approved by the highest court of the State whose people are directly concerned, that it will interfere with the action of such authority only when it is plain and palpable that it has no real or substantial relation to the public health, safety, morals, or to the general welfare.

Metzenbaum was hopeful that the High Court would follow its own precedent by reconfirming this deferential standard.

Metzenbaum's "Conclusion" was a historical excursion through American regulation of urban land uses in which (1) nuisance law—judge-made and then statutory—featured prominently, and (2) it became apparent that the statutory solutions to meet the challenges of the increasing complexities of urban life were modern necessities justified by the police power. In the beginning, "when the Country was in its early state, the powder mill, the inn, the houses and the primitive stores were clustered together in 'Town Centers.'" The powder mill was relocated to "a more outlying district" when the population grew, followed by "ostracism" as "'Common Law' Nuisances." Because the "public welfare" needed more expansive protection, "there then began to appear, year by year, a great variety of enactments against what has come to be commonly called 'Statutory' nuisances," banning such uses as brick kilns, livery stables, and public laundries from residential districts.

Metzenbaum then described the acceptance of "Tenement Housing Codes" in New York by which property owners "who always believed they could build upon their land with such buildings and in such manner as they chose because they were the owners of their land and were protected therein by the Federal and State Constitutions" suddenly "found themselves confronted with enactments which minutely regulated the building and construction." Next, investigations by "Sanitarians, Engineers, and the Medical Profession" justified area restrictions, as "it became evident that unless buildings were denied the right to occupy more than a portion of their respective lots, light and sunshine and natural benefits would be thwarted and the health and safety of the community would, to that extent, be injured and reduced." The result was the authorization of building codes in all states, and, Metzenbaum exclaimed with some hyperbole, "today there is no hamlet so small or so poor as not to have its thorough and exacting" version. Once again, despite property owners' insistence that their constitutional rights were being violated, "the Federal as well as the courts of last resort of every state have pronounced these codes to be legal and within the Police Power."

Height restriction was the next item on the regulatory agenda, for "a new menace was darkening the horizon by reason of the construction of very high buildings, which added their congestion to the streets, which darkened the thoroughfares and which shut out the light from adjoining and nearby buildings." Once again, "the Police Power — always equal to the occasion of protecting the public welfare against new conditions as they arise — was once more invoked in the way of enactments which limited the *height* of buildings and which regulated them for the public safety." Similarly, "Fire Zone" laws were justified and approved, despite the complaints of those inside the zone that property owners on the outside were not required to spend money to comply with the extra requirements.

Realities on the ground justified this modern approach to land-use regulation. Metzenbaum explained, in words that would eventually be echoed in Justice Sutherland's opinion by the Supreme Court, that these and other statutory changes "were occasioned by new and unfolding conditions and were necessitated by reason of greater complexity in Civil life, a greater realization of the need to protect the public health, the vitality of the nation, the safety of it people and the welfare of its children as well as the conservation of its property." While not needed in the "early or colonial days," these additional steps became necessary "and appropriate by reason of the increasing population, the manifest congestion, the intensiveness of American life and the new ills which sprang from these new conditions." What was true of nuisance statutes, tenement and building codes, height restrictions, and fire zones was also true of the "use districts" found in zoning ordinances.

Appended to Metzenbaum's first brief were statistics from the U.S. Department of Commerce noting that "by the first of July of this year [1925] more than 26,000,000 people were living in 366 zoned municipalities as against the less than 11,000,000 people in 48 cities and towns in September 1921," and that "forty-four out of the sixty-eight largest cities in the United States, with a population of more than one hundred thousand, have zoning ordinances in effect." The message was anything but subtle: to affirm Judge Westenhaver's decision would have a dramatic and immediate impact on the quality of life of millions of Americans. The final word in Metzenbaum's copious brief was reserved for Commerce Secretary Hoover himself, who, in an address before the National Association of Real Estate Boards, bemoaned the fact that nearly 60 percent of Americans were tenants. "Nothing is worse than an increased tenantry and landlordism in this country," he exclaimed. What was the solution? "The municipalities through the enactment of wise zoning laws should cooperate." In closing, Hoover explained, using rhetoric that, in the twenty-first century, would be deemed an endorsement of "intergenerational equity":

> This country of ours is still in the making. Shall we look forward as far-sighted empire builders to the conditions which will confront our children in another 20 or 30 years, or shall we as shortsighted, greedy opportunists exploit the present without regard to future consequences?

To Metzenbaum and the supporters of zoning, the stakes were quite high.

Baker and Morgan's weighty brief in response stressed the economic impact of zoning on Ambler Realty's 68-acre tract and provided a detailed description of Euclid's "so-called zoning ordinance." Baker and Morgan distilled the conflict down to one basic question: "whether Ordinance No. 2812 of the Village of Euclid, as amended, is a valid police regulation of the property of the appellee in the village." Instead of "pursu[ing] any rational plan, dictated by considerations of public safety, health and welfare upon which the police power rests," the "ordinance is an arbitrary attempt to prevent the natural and proper development of the land in the village prejudicial to the public welfare, in that it prohibits the business and industry of the metropolitan district of Cleveland from access to land economically most available." The appellee landowner agreed with the appellant village that height and area restrictions, building codes, and regulations controlling "density of use" "in the interest of the public safety, health, morals and welfare, are propositions long since established." Moreover, "equally well established" was the proposition "that a rational use of this [municipal] power may be made by dividing a municipality into districts or zones, and varying the requirements according to the characteristics of the districts." However, the municipal powers "must be reasonably exercised," and local officials "may not, under the guise of the police power, arbitrarily divert property from its appropriate and most economical uses or diminish its value by imposing restrictions which have no other basis than the momentary taste of the public authorities." Justice Sutherland's opinion would accept the reasonable and arbitrary standards, but ultimately reject the landowner's characterization of government abuse.

The former mayor of Cleveland, not surprisingly, attempted to direct the Court's attention to the metropolitan impact of zoning controls:

> The municipal limits of the Village of Euclid are, after all, arbitrary and accidental political lines. The metropolitan city of Cleveland is one of the great industrial centers of the United States. If the Village of Euclid may lawfully prefer to remain rural and restrict the normal industrial and business development of its

land, each of the other municipalities, circumadjacent to the City of Cleveland, may pursue a like course.

Modern proponents of a regional approach to planning specifically, and governance generally, could not have stated the matter more succinctly.

If zoning was not about the protection of public health, safety, morals, and general welfare, then why, according to Baker and Morgan, were American towns and cities so anxious to use this tool, to the detriment of private property rights? The answer was simple, and disturbing:

> Even if the world could agree by unanimous consent upon what is beautiful and desirable, it could not, under our constitutional theory, enforce its decision by prohibiting a land owner, who refuses to accept the world's view of beauty, from making otherwise safe and innocent uses of his land. . . . The world has not reached a unanimous judgment about beauty, and there are few unlikelier places to look for stable judgments on such subjects than in the changing discretion of legislative bodies. . . . We respectfully submit that counsel for appellant, in his fervor for an extension of the police power which will permit municipalities to accomplish all the great goods at which zoning aims, overlooks the fact that, after all, this is merely a desire of some people to tell other people how to use their property.

In opposition to Metzenbaum's (and Hoover's) arguments about the overriding public benefit, counsel for the appellee attempted to return the Court to first principles of freedom and individuality. "The theory of our liberty has always been to maintain the right of the individual to his liberty and to his property," they wrote, "and to allow free play to economic laws, private contract and personal choice." The most conservative members on the Supreme Court could not have expressed this basic, conservative notion more artfully.

Baker and Morgan reviewed the law from other jurisdictions, emphasizing antizoning decisions from states such as Texas, Maryland, and New Jersey, and the apparently conflicting Ohio cases.

Applying the law to the facts of the case led Ambler Realty's counsel to the conclusion that their client had suffered a real harm without legal justification: "The existence of Ordinance No. 2812 and the implications of power claimed by its enactment are the cause of the wrong and damage to the appellee." As a good Progressive, Baker would "admit that as human progress develops, new conditions may arise and new discoveries be made that will cause new conceptions of social needs and bring within the legislative power fields previously not occupied." But, such was not the case with Euclid's zoning ordinance: "we frankly do not believe that there has been any such development of new conditions as necessitates or justifies the communal control of private property attempted by this ordinance, or by many others, some of which have been sustained by state courts." Counsel for Ambler Realty asked whether the Court would really be willing to stretch constitutional principles this far.

On Wednesday, January 27, 1926, only a few days after Baker and Morgan filed their brief, eight justices participated in oral arguments in the old Senate chamber. An article in the *Christian Science Monitor*, published a few weeks later, provided a description of the setting and the procedures for the Supreme Court's October 1925 Term. The article, entitled "Supreme Court Sessions Opened by Centuries-Old Cry of 'Oyez,'" explained that, while Monday was set aside for the publication of opinions, the rest of the week, including Friday, was devoted to oral arguments. Convening at noon, the Supreme Court sat "in a chamber adjacent to the Senate side of the Capitol, where formerly the Senate met. This was before the congressional wings were added to the Capitol in 1859." In 1929, at the urging of Chief Justice Taft, Congress authorized the construction of the permanent building for the Court, which was completed six years later. Not surprisingly (given Taft's historical association with the City Beautiful movement), the new Court building, designed by beaux arts architect Cass Gilbert, would be one of the last neoclassical buildings erected in the capital city during the 1930s.

The layout of the room in which cases were heard before the move was described thus:

Chief Justice Taft is seated in the center, the eight justices being arranged on either side of him, in order of seniority. Before the court is a row of tables for attorneys and litigants. Then a row of seats for newspaper men, and then the places for spectators.

On the day that *Euclid v. Ambler* was first argued, however, only eight justices were present. George Sutherland, who was named in 1922 by his friend Warren G. Harding to replace Justice Clarke, was not present. In fact, according to the "Daily Legal Record" kept by the *Washington Post*, while Justice Sutherland was on the bench for the first four public sessions in 1926 (January 2 through January 8), he did not sit with his brethren from January 11 through February 1, 1927, for a total of nine missed public sessions. The reasons for his absence are unclear, although a short Associated Press news article dated January 30 reported that Justice Sutherland was in Charleston, South Carolina, along with his wife. "He has declined invitations to address local clubs on the ground that he is enjoying a respite from all work." Whatever health or other issue was keeping the absent justice from his work was resolved by March 1, 1926, when he again joined the Court in public session.

We cannot know for sure what was said during oral argument on January 27, as neither party requested a transcript (Baker, for one, chose not to pay the sixty-dollar fee to a shorthand reporter who solicited Baker's business in a letter sent the day of the argument). However, the *Cleveland Plain Dealer* provided a detailed account of the give and take with the justices. Metzenbaum began the proceedings by informing the Court that thirty-one states had passed zoning enabling acts and that the village had the authority under Ohio law to limit its industrial areas. He insisted that there was adequate industrial acreage between the two railroad lines and Euclid Avenue to meet the needs articulated by the experts who spoke in opposition to the ordinance. He attempted to provide key statistical details:

> The village of Euclid now has a population of 10,000, and an area of sixteen square miles. One-fifth of the total area is zoned for industrial purposes. There is [*sic*] fourteen miles of railroad frontage, unrestricted, available for industrial purposes, yet there are only sixteen industries of all kinds in that area. But eight of these are large ones.

Moreover, Metzenbaum emphasized that the ordinance actually enhanced property values and cited state decisions from Ohio and several other states in support of zoning.

Thanks to newspaper accounts and to Metzenbaum's 1930 treatise on zoning, we can recreate this humorous exchange that took place during the appellants' argument:

> CHIEF JUSTICE TAFT: What is the difference between a "realtor" and a "real estate man"?
> METZENBAUM: I don't know. I have been using them interchangeably to avoid using the same word twice.
> JUSTICE HOLMES: I believe we learned here the other day that a "realtor" charges a man a higher rate than a "real estate man."
> CHIEF JUSTICE TAFT (chuckling and leaning back in his chair): That's about the same difference there is between a statesman and a politician.

Holmes might have been correct. Technically, however, the term "realtor" (which since 1949 has carried a trademark) referred at the time to members of the National Association of Real Estate Boards, an organization of real estate agents (or "real estate men") who subscribed to a special code of ethics.

Metzenbaum was also asked to respond to arguments raised by a friend of the court in support of the village, but that were cited by opposing counsel Baker:

> METZENBAUM: The citations were not from my brief. They were from *amicus curiae*, persons who entered this case as friends of the court. I don't blame them for attempting to save the nation, considering my impotence.
> CHIEF JUSTICE TAFT: You want to be saved from your friends?
> METZENBAUM: That is it exactly.

Apparently, Metzenbaum was not yet ready to concede command in this battle to those fellow combatants who rose in defense of zoning.

It was apparent from the beginning of Baker's argument that the two advocates were operating on parallel planes. Rather than countering Metzenbaum's assertions regarding zoning as a national phenomenon widely endorsed by experts and the courts, Baker attempted to shift the Court's focus to the plight of his client: "I do not assume the burden of declaring generally and completely the invalidity of all controlling ordinances. I am not going to indulge in abstract philosophy on the subject." Baker, using the map that was placed on a frame before the bench, chose instead "to deal with the particular effect of this case on the community and show that it is arbitrary, unreasonable and not in good faith so far as my clients are concerned."

While Metzenbaum painted a picture of Euclid as an independent entity, Baker took a metropolitan approach, portraying Cleveland as "a fan shaped city" that "is completely circuited by a continuous group of separate municipalities." One of those municipalities was Euclid—"a residence section for the people of Cleveland." City and suburb were inextricably linked: "Its water supply and street systems are harmonious with those of Cleveland. No one can consider its [Euclid's] welfare as distinct from the metropolitan area."

Counsel for Ambler Realty grabbed the attention of the chief justice, a fellow Ohioan, when Baker discussed the dramatic transformation of Euclid Avenue from a residential to a business street. "I used to know Cleveland well in the early '80s," Taft responded, "and I was there recently and I would not have recognized it as the same city." Baker then speculated that if Cleveland had designated Euclid Avenue a residential zone when he arrived in the city in 1899, this move would have changed the entire course of the city's growth. In the same manner, Euclid was attempting, according to the news story, "to put on a straitjacket that may seriously interfere with the development of the Cleveland metropolitan district in the future." In this way, Baker was reiterating one of Judge Westenhaver's chief themes.

Although he avoided "abstract philosophy," Baker did mix in a little theory with a worst-case scenario: "We must consider the effect if each one of these villages shall pass restrictions solely without regard to the whole. The operation of natural and economic laws should be permitted." The Court should not allow "every village council and local influence" to interfere with these "laws." After this informative and at times humorous session, the eight justices took the case under advisement.

Metzenbaum was deeply troubled by his opponent's performance, particularly the last fifteen minutes (out of the allotted one hour), during which, according to Metzenbaum's version, "the attention of the members of the court was invited by counsel for the complainant, to a recitation which the writer felt to be at distinct variance with the facts as adduced by the testimony and as contained in the ordinance itself." Metzenbaum restrained himself, however, as "neither good breeding nor proper court decorum would permit of any interruption or spoken challenge."

That night was a restless one for Metzenbaum as he planned to head back to Cleveland by rail. Fearful that the winds had shifted in Ambler Realty's favor during the final crucial minutes of Baker's oral argument, Metzenbaum had decided that, upon his arrival back in Ohio, he would telephone an attorney in Washington with directions to contact the Supreme Court on Friday morning with a request to grant Metzenbaum an opportunity to respond by brief to Baker's disturbing and misleading argument. The timing was crucial, because Friday, January 29, would be the last day of business for the Court before the justices took a break until Monday, March 1.

Speaking of winds, the weather took a dramatic turn for the worse as Metzenbaum headed west. The banner headline across the front page of the *Cleveland Plain Dealer* on January 29 read, "Zero Gale Slashes over Ohio," and the paper reported that the state "was virtually snowbound yesterday, after one of the worst blizzards in years." When Metzenbaum realized that the severe delays caused by snow on the rails would spoil his initial plan to seek to the Court's permission, he placed his hope in this telegram that he sent to the chief justice while on the way home:

ENROUTE TO CLEVELAND JAN 29 1926
HON CHIEF JUSTICE WILLIAM H TAFT
CARE THE SUPREME COURT WASHINGTON DC
IN AMBLE[R] AGAINST VILLAGE OF EUCLID IT IS FELT THAT VILLAGE OUGHT TO FILE A REPLY BRIEF TO ANSWER CONCLUDING PORTION OF AMBLER ORAL ARGUMENT AND OF AMBLER BRIEF STOP WANTED TO ASK THIS PRIVILEGE WHILE IN YOUR COURT BUT HESITATED REGARDING PROPRIETY THERE OF STOP AFTER REFLECTING UPON IMPORTANCE OF CAUSE AND GREAT PUBLIC

INTEREST AND NOT FOR ANY MERE PERSONAL DESIRE TO WIN
FEEL CONSCIOUS DU[T]Y WOULD NOT BE FULFILLED UNLESS
REQUEST IS MADE TO FILE SHORT REPLY BRIEF WITHIN SUCH TIME
AS YOU MAY STIPULATE STOP AMBLER BRIEF WAS SERVED AND
FILED SO FEW DAYS BEFORE HEARING THAT REPLY BRIEF WAS
QUITE IMPOSSIBLE INTENDED TELEPHONING WASHINGTON
ATTORNEY TO APPEAR AND MOVE THIS REQUEST BUT THAT WILL
BE IMPOSSIBLE BECAUSE PREVAILING STORM HAS DELAYED TRAIN
SO MANY HOURS TRAIN WILL NOT ARRIVE IN CLEVELAND IN TIME
TO PERMIT TELEPHONING AND APPEARANCE WHEN COURT OPENS
STOP UNDERSTAND TODAY IS LAST SESSION BEFORE COURT
RECESSES AND THEREFORE TAKE THIS MANNER OF MAKING APPLI-
CATION PLEASE FORGIVE THIS METHOD OF REQUEST AS NO LACK
OF RESPECT OR VIOLATION OF RULES IS INTENDED RESPECTFULLY
THE VILLAGE OF EUCLID
BY JAMES METZENBAUM

Some years after the event, in his treatise on zoning, Metzenbaum
would include a slightly revised version of the message in which, for
example, he had explained that he was "compelled by conscientious
duty." He also included this memorable description of the manner in
which he dispatched the telegram form:

> As the train slowed down along a siding where a great string of
> freight cars were being shoveled out of the snow, I opened the
> door of the car in which I was riding, leaned out from the car plat-
> form and shouted to one of the men who was engaged in the work
> of shoveling; wrapping the money around the telegram and toss-
> ing it to him. I saw it light on a great bank of snow. This was done
> with the trust that the man would understand what was wanted.

Metzenbaum's trust was rewarded, as Taft sent the following reply
on February 2: "The court allows you one week in which to file reply
brief and serve it upon your opponent, and gives him a week in which
to reply to yours, after service. Please advise opposing counsel of this
telegram."

This may have been an instance in which the medium was more
important than the message, however. The case file, currently housed

in the National Archives, reveals that, for the long period in which *Euclid v. Ambler* was before the Supreme Court, Metzenbaum was continually bombarding the clerk's office with one request after another on issues major and, more often, quite minor. His angst was often palpable. In a letter dated November 4, 1925, for example, Metzenbaum wrote:

> Frankly, I have begun to worry lest I may not have this Brief in on time and so I am taking liberty of once more troubling you to ask in reference to this phase of the subject.
>
> If the Brief reaches your hands by the latter part of this month — November — will that be in sufficient time or must I have it in by the middle of this month?
>
> I will not procrastinate or delay even though I know that I will have time until the latter part of this month, but, on the contrary, if I do have that knowledge, then it will relieve me of the mental fear of having this cause stricken from the files and records because the Brief has not been submitted in time.
>
> At the present moment I fear that I am working "against time," and this really keeps me distressed and troubled, because I want to do my very best and because I want to make the presentation as perfect as it lies within my power to do and so I am trustful that I may have until the latter part of this month without any fear that this will mean possible rejection of the entire cause by the Court.

The clerk's office's reply dated the following day gave the nervous counsel some breathing space: "This case will not be reached in November or December, as I thought when you last requested this information, and it will probably go over until the latter part of January." There were many similar exchanges that took place between 1924 and 1926.

One such exchange of letters occurred on August 19 and 21 of 1925. Among several inquiries that Metzenbaum had for the clerk was the following, "Is it permitted to file a Reply Brief after the other side has filed its Answering Brief?" The clerk's office responded, "The filing of a reply brief is permitted under the rules here." When the chief justice informed village counsel that he would have a chance to respond to Baker and Morgan's brief, it was actually a confirmation of information that Metzenbaum had received months before. It thus appears that the snowy drama may have been unnecessary to accomplish his immediate goal.

The pace of work in Metzenbaum's office in the Hickox Building on Euclid Avenue in Cleveland must have been frantic, because the reply brief was drafted and printed on time. Metzenbaum's concern with the substance of Baker's oral argument permeated the fifty-three page document. For example, early on, Metzenbaum wrote:

> Though we have no stenographic record of the oral argument before the Supreme Court, it prominently stands out in our recollection for The Ambler Company, in the very opening sentences, asserted that the Complainant was not so much insisting upon the fundamental principle of unconstitutionality of Zoning and Districting ordinances, but was primarily relying upon the unconstitutionality of this ordinance in respect to its application to the particular parcel belonging to the Complainant. This apparent reversal of the importance of the two questions, makes it important that the question of damage be definitely determined and for that purpose we beg the indulgence by the Court.

Because Baker and Morgan had highlighted the economic impact of Euclid's ordinance on Ambler Realty's parcel, Metzenbaum devoted several pages to disputing the landowner's analysis, the accuracy of its witnesses' statements in the trial court, and the presentation of these issues in the appellee's brief. In the midst of a sustained, multi-front attack on Ambler Realty's tactics, Metzenbaum assured the justices that "our earnest esteem for the Ambler counsel is not one whit diminished; for our affectionate regard, of so long standing, really grows warmer year by year."

On the heels of this curious, but most likely sincere, disclaimer, Metzenbaum introduced a litany of misstatements that Baker allegedly made during his one-hour presentation on January 27. For example, Metzenbaum asserted that near the close of Baker's argument, the landowner's counsel "referred to the fact that the ordinance apparently denied the right to establish orphanages along the high side of Euclid Avenue and feelingly referred to the denial of the right to use this 'leafy hillside' for the orphaned young." Metzenbaum claimed that he "sat in amazement as he heard the Ambler company present a picture which was diametrically opposite to the testimony which the Ambler counsel themselves had brought into the Record."

Thanks to Metzenbaum's reply brief, the reader can gain some insights as to Baker's ample skills as a creative appellate advocate. Apparently, with his words Baker presented to the Court a vivid visual image: "the painting of the complainant standing upon the site of its present acreage and seeing the approach of factories along the north side of Euclid Avenue and the smoke coming toward the Village and then the purchase of the sixty-eight acres by the complainant." The evident purpose of this "painting" was to convince the Court that the use of the parcel for industrial purposes was inevitable if not for the intrusive and confiscatory government ordinance. Metzenbaum felt "entitled to recite the facts required to aid the Court in seeing the *real* situation"—a situation in which "no factory or industry throughout the entire Village comes near to Euclid Avenue as is permitted by the ordinance," and "that if one were to start at the Public Square in the City of Cleveland where Euclid Avenue begins and were to walk eastwardly" for 30 miles, through the central city and the eastern suburbs, there would be only three industrial uses, none of which was in Euclid itself. Although Metzenbaum conceded that the "oral picture" was "impressive," it was not factual.

We also learn from Metzenbaum's reply brief of Baker's "attempt to belittle the Village by referring to its having wrapped about itself an oversized coat." Village counsel's rejoinder was that, "unlike garments of cloth, the Constitution of the United States automatically fits and equally applies to large and small" — to the relatively modest hamlet of Euclid and to the "great corporation" of Gotham itself, New York City. Both are entitled to use zoning ordinances "so as to prevent injury and so as to bring forth the greatest public welfare." The constitutional police power came in one size that fit all municipalities.

At the end of what Metzenbaum thought was his final attempt to convince the Court of the justness of his cause, he addressed Ambler Realty's allegation that it had suffered damage as a result of the passage of the zoning ordinance. Metzenbaum denied that a landowner had the right to prevail if it could demonstrate that "its property can not be used for what it conceives to be its greatest advantage," that is, to maximize the profit on its investment in real estate. Even if Ambler Realty could not use the property to "its greatest advantage," and even if (theoretically) the landowner has suffered "some loss or damage," that could not "be the sole or final test, for if the inhibition of the use is or could be related to public welfare and safety, then the damage (even if there were such) would need to yield to the public good." That was the holding in cases involving height restrictions and other valid police power regulations, including zoning cases from several state courts.

Metzenbaum, who asserted "that the ordinance actually *enhanced* the value" of Ambler Realty's parcel, was not taking any chances that, despite his argument about the public good, the more conservative justices would fall for Baker and Morgan's claim that their client had suffered damage. Village counsel laid out twelve pairs (labeled "a" through "l") of allegedly unfounded claims and refutations. Two examples follow:

(b) The Bill [of Complaint] alleged that factories had lodges along Euclid Avenue, But

The proof of the complainant as well as the Defendant shows that no factory has come so near to Euclid Avenue as is permitted by the ordinance.

(i) The Bill alleges that the zoning ordinance was established for mere aesthetic reasons and was designed to keep the Village as a residential municipality, But

The proof shows that 1400 acres (substantially more than one-fifth of the Village) are open and awaiting industrial development. . . .

The reply brief closed with an update on recent developments in the courts, noting that Judge Westenhaver's holding in the case two years before had not gained acceptance in state courts. Metzenbaum reiterated that thirty-one states and hundreds of cities, large and small, were part of the zoning phenomenon. As a result, many Americans "trustfully look forward to a final vindication by the highest

Court of their land." If persistence plus zeal equaled success then the village would get its "vindication."

Baker and Morgan, not surprisingly, were not ready to give up the struggle on behalf of their client and, by extension, other landowners who viewed zoning as an invalid and confiscatory expansion of the police power. In the appellee's reply brief, counsel dismissed Metzenbaum's allegation that Judge Westenhaver had "disposed of this case upon an inadequate consideration of the evidence." To the contrary, "the trial judge lives in Cleveland and knows the situation," as well as the witnesses, and the "physical situation" of the burgeoning, industrial central city and its suburbs. Ambler Realty remained confident in asserting that the village of Euclid had exceeded its authority under the police power; that the provisions of the village zoning ordinance were "arbitrary, irrational and confiscatory," and not in good faith; and that the operation of the ordinance "upon the lands of the plaintiff has destroyed their salability," with the result "that the plaintiff's market for its land is destroyed and a substantial part of the value of its land is confiscated." Baker and Morgan disputed in great detail Metzenbaum's argument regarding the damage suffered by their client.

Nearly half of the forty-two printed pages of the appellee's reply brief were devoted to a comparison of Euclid's residential restrictions with those found in zoning ordinances from Denver, Rochester (New York), Evanston (Illinois), Washington, D.C., Detroit, Omaha, Pittsburgh, Milwaukee, Seattle, and Baltimore. The conclusion that Baker and Morgan drew from this exercise was that "the Village of Euclid imposes far more burdensome restrictions and devotes more than half of its area to single family residences, while it thrusts apartment houses, hotels, clubs, churches and banks, to say nothing of retail drygoods and grocery and drug stores, down either into or immediately adjacent to the district declared by it appropriate for heavy industrial uses."

The appellee was suggesting an alternative route for the Supreme Court to take, should the justices feel uncomfortable in bucking the state court trend of approving zoning in theory. The High Court could simply declare this one zoning ordinance beyond the pale, because of the extreme protections it afforded the single-family home. In any event, Baker and Morgan were asking the justices to affirm the trial court's finding that Euclid's entire zoning ordinance, in its current iteration, was invalid. Should the Supreme Court follow this course, village officials would be free to pursue legislative changes that "it deems in the public interest after it has been advised of the protection afforded by the Constitution of the United States to the rights of private property." After a second round of briefing, the parties remained sharply divided as to two key issues — (1) the amount of damage, if any, suffered by Ambler Realty, and (2) the character of Euclid's ordinance as compared with its counterparts throughout the nation.

When the Supreme Court reconvened on Monday, March 1, Chief Justice Taft dropped a bombshell on the participants who were awaiting a decision when he announced, "This case is remanded to the docket for a reargument and assigned for October 4" (the date would later be pushed back a week). For decades, lawyers and historians have speculated on the reasons for the Court's unusual, though certainly not unprecedented, decision to rehear the case. Suspicion has generally focused on two actors: Justice Harlan Fiske Stone and Alfred Bettman.

The Stone theory can be traced to an article that appeared in the *Columbia Law Review* in 1946, five years after Stone was elevated to the position of chief justice. The author was Alfred McCormack, who had served as Associate Justice Stone's clerk for the October, 1925 Term (Stone's first full session). This term included of course the initial oral argument for *Euclid v. Ambler* in January 1926. In his discussion of Stone's influence on the Court's decisions, even early in his career on the High Court, McCormack provided the following example:

> In those days there was no premium on dissents. Even Holmes and Brandeis, the great dissenters, sometimes refrained from noting disagreement in cases where their individual votes had been adverse; it was not uncommon for dissenters to continue the argument with the judge who was writing the opinion, after the decision in the case had been reached. Occasionally they were successful. Justice Sutherland, for instance, was writing an opinion for the majority in *Village of Euclid v. Ambler Realty Co.*, holding the zoning ordinance unconstitutional, when talks with this dis-

senting brethren (principally Stone, I believe) shook his convictions and led him to request a reargument, after which he changed his mind and the ordinance was upheld.

Ten years later, Stone's biographer, Alpheus Thomas Mason, retold and embellished McCormack's story, writing that Stone, who engaged in "persistent hammering" of the justice from Utah, was "instrumental" in Sutherland's "shift." This version of the events has continued to circulate to this day.

The McCormack account is problematic for a few important reasons. First, Justice Sutherland was not present at oral argument on January 27; indeed he was not listed as present at the public sessions from January 11 through February 1, after which the Court took a one-month hiatus. While Sutherland did not recuse himself from the cases that were argued in his absence during that period, it would have been highly unusual, if not unique, for the chief justice to assign the majority opinion to Sutherland under those circumstances.

Second, Metzenbaum's request to write a reply brief was granted on February 2. Why would the chief justice have assigned anyone to write a draft opinion in the case before the Court heard first from Metzenbaum and then Baker? It is also highly unlikely that, had Sutherland waited until he received the briefs in mid-February, he would have drafted an opinion for at least five justices, circulated the draft, conferred with Stone or any other colleague on the Court, and changed his mind, all before March 1, the day on which Taft announced the rehearing.

Third, there is good evidence that in 1925, a year before the first oral argument, Sutherland was not strongly opposed to the concept of zoning. In reality, *Euclid v. Ambler* was not the first comprehensive zoning case to be placed on the Supreme Court's docket. On April 25, 1925, the Court heard arguments in *New York* ex rel. *Rosevale Realty Co. v. Kleinert*, a landowner's challenge to New York City's monumental 1916 Building Zone Resolution. The state courts had denied relief to Rosevale Realty, so Rosevale filed a petition for writ of error with the Supreme Court, in which the company asserted that the "resolution was unconstitutional and deprived [the landowner] of property without due process of law and contravened the 14th Amendment to the Constitution of the United States." Unfortunately for Rosevale, its counsel had not made arguments based on violations of the *federal* Constitution in the state courts. As a result, in a unanimous opinion written by Justice Edward Terry Sanford, the Supreme Court concluded that, because there was no "federal question" for the justices to decide, it was necessary to dismiss the writ "without consideration of the merits" of the landowner's allegations. Thanks to Professor Robert Post's detective work, we know that, while the *Rosevale Realty* case was still pending before the High Court, Sutherland had sent to the Chief Justice a memorandum summarizing his positions on several cases. About the New York zoning case, Sutherland wrote, "In the modern development of cities and towns, zoning laws are universally recognized as necessary and proper. The question presented by the law under review is a matter of degree, and I am not prepared to say that the judgment of the local law-makers was arbitrarily exercised. Affirm." These words indicate that, if a shift ever occurred, it did so before the justices discussed the zoning dispute in Euclid, Ohio.

There is a second, contemporary source that confirms a division on the Court and an important role for Stone, yet not the role about which McCormack speculated ("principally Stone, I believe"). On May 22, 1926, zoning opponent George T. Simpson sent a letter to Baker in which the Minnesota lawyer (and former state attorney general) relayed the story of a conversation that another lawyer had had with Justice Louis D. Brandeis's secretary, in which it was reported that the decision to hear a second argument in the case was attributable to "the fact that the court was so closely divided that neither side dared risk a vote." The letter puts Brandeis and Holmes in the pro-zoning category, James Clark McReynolds, Willis Van Devanter, and Pierce Butler in opposition, and the Chief Justice "an uncertain quantity." Stone was described as "a new member who was not fully conversant with the situation, and who desired more time that he may acquaint himself." Simpson told Baker, "I got the impression from what he said that the reargument was made at Stone's suggestion." This version seems more accurate, particularly because, with the benefit of 20-20 hindsight, we know that the voting alliances were correct, and because it indicates that no vote had been taken before March 1. While this second-hand account converts Stone from a "hammerer" to a "suggester," McCormack can be excused for reading backward from Stone's eventual strong presence on the Court to the justice's first full term sixteen years before.

That Alfred Bettman played a significant role in carrying the day for the forces of zoning is almost undeniable. Whether he is the hero of the struggle is still subject to debate. The strongest case for attributing to the Cincinnati lawyer and to the national planning movement the Court's decision to rehear *Euclid v. Ambler* appeared in *The Planning Function in Urban Government*, a 1941 study by Robert Averill Walker. According to Walker's version of the events, after the adverse holding in the trial court, the leadership of the National Conference on City Planning was divided over whether to file an *amicus curiae* brief in support of the constitutionality of zoning. On one side were those who believed "that the facts in the Euclid case were such as to make an adverse decision almost inevitable, and, therefore, that the conference should not attempt to uphold it." On the other side were those, "including Alfred Bettman of Cincinnati, [who] took the position that this would be a vital decision and that every effort should be made to secure a favorable verdict." Bettman's side prevailed, and "it was arranged that Mr. Bettman would submit a brief on behalf of the conference."

These arrangements nearly fell through, however, owing to an oversight by the otherwise heroic Bettman. The "Revised Rules of the Supreme Court of the United States," which went into effect on July 1, 1925, clearly provided, "No brief will be received through the clerk or otherwise after a case has been argued or submitted, except upon special leave granted in open court after notice to opposing counsel." When, in February 1926, Bettman wrote to the clerk of the Supreme Court to find out if the oral argument had taken place, he found out that the argument had and that it was too late to file his brief. On the clerk's suggestion, Bettman wrote his fellow Cincinnattian, Chief Justice Taft, who later that month invited the submission of the brief. Following the Court's new rules, Taft announced in "open court" on October 11, 1926, one day before the case was argued a second time, that leave was formally granted to the National Conference to file a brief.

From this chronology, Walker made a tentative leap toward a solution to the reargument puzzle: "It cannot be asserted dogmatically that the rehearing was solely for the purpose of letting Mr.

Bettman's brief in, but the correspondence was about the brief, and the latter seems to have been the only new element introduced." Walker also repeated the rumor that "it is understood that a divided court had decided against the validity of comprehensive zoning by one vote following the first hearing." This story makes for good drama, complete with a flawed champion who received a last-minute reprieve and then made the argument that resulted in a new majority.

In reality, between January 26 and March 1, there were other "elements," in addition to Bettman's letter (not yet a brief), for the Court to consider. Initially, there was Metzenbaum's desperate attempt to correct the (mis)impressions that Baker made on the Court during the closing minutes of the first oral argument, a countering move that paid off in the grant of permission to file new briefs. Second, there were the two new briefs themselves. These documents indicated that the first set of briefs and the oral argument had done little to clarify the muddy issues regarding the constitutionality of zoning, the state of the law nationally, the economic impact of the ordinance on Ambler Realty, and the exact breadth of Ambler Realty's lawsuit (whether it was an attack on all zoning or on the reasonableness of one ordinance as enacted). When we add these developments to the divisions among the justices, and consider the important fact that one member of the Court missed the oral argument, reargument seems to be a logical and only mildly surprising step for the Taft Court to have taken.

Metzenbaum and Baker did not rest once their briefs had been swiftly completed and submitted. The July 1926, issue of *The American City* magazine carried an article by the former on "Zoning on Trial before the U.S. Supreme Court." Metzenbaum warned his readers that, if Judge Westenhaver's decision that zoning "takes" property without compensation should be affirmed, "then zoning throughout *all* states will necessarily fall, because of course the Federal constitution applies to all states, and for the further reason that state constitutions contain virtually the same inhibition." To this nonlegal audience, Metzenbaum presented a point that he had been stressing in his briefs: His goal was for the 30 million Americans who reside in municipalities with zoning to receive a ruling from the highest court in the land "that the basic and fundamental theory of zoning, as expressed in the usual comprehensive zoning ordinance is legal, valid, and constitutional." After all, the village could "well afford to amend its ordinance if the Supreme Court should hold it to be unreasonable in its effect upon the parcel in question, for that is of comparatively small moment." Metzenbaum, in his first (and ultimately only) case before the Supreme Court, was not hiding his ambitious agenda.

As for the justices' choice to hear another set of oral arguments in the dispute, Metzenbaum reported that newspapers had attributed the rehearing decision to the fact that the Court was "disinclined to decide important questions upon a closely divided basis." Metzenbaum wrote that he had "no means of knowing if there is any division of opinion among the Supreme Court justices, nor whether such division (if it does exist)" referred to the fundamental constitutional question or the narrow issue of the reasonableness of the ordinance as it affected one parcel. All Metzenbaum could surmise from the March 1 announcement was "that our highest Federal Court is apparently unwilling to immediately or summarily agree with the ruling of the trial court."

The village's counsel was active outside of the public view as well. In September 1926, Metzenbaum sent a telegram to A. J. Hill, an attorney who was challenging the city of Los Angeles in a case that would be decided in the city's favor the following year. Metzenbaum requested from Hill a transcript of part of Baker's first oral argument in *Euclid v. Ambler* that was in Hill's possession. The telegraph read, "Several places but particularly near opening Baker stated principal objection was unconstitutionality because of unreasonableness as applied to Ambler parcel and not because of unconstitutionality of all zoning ordinances." Hill complied with Metzenbaum's request and informed Baker that he had done so. In reply, Baker wrote that "the extract . . . seems to me to be innocuous and I shall not be terrified at meeting it again." He would reencounter his own words at least once, in Metzenbaum's final brief.

Baker's contact with Hill was part of a set of correspondence with other attorneys who were active in the nationwide battle against zoning. In fact, that same September, Hill had attempted to convince the Court to advance his Los Angeles case so that it could be heard with *Euclid v. Ambler* the following month. Baker predicted, wrongly as it turned out, that the justices would agree to merge the two challenges. He welcomed that strategy, noting, "It will be better for the court to have as many phases of this omnibus power before it as possible." In contrast to Baker's hopes, the Court from 1926 to 1928 would hear various zoning cases one by one, not all at once.

Baker engaged in an effort to enlist other like-minded attorneys to file *amicus* briefs to oppose "the 'zoners' [who] will file poetic and romantic disquisitions on behalf of the principle by which they think they are going to solve all the problems of society and ultimately produce a better and handsomer human race." In December 1925, in a response to a letter from a Baltimore attorney reporting on a recent Maryland court ruling, Baker expressed these candid concerns about the theory and practice of zoning:

> The more experience I have had with zoning ordinances, . . . the more satisfied I am that the whole theory is wrong. Nobody knows enough or can know enough to zone a city. As a matter of fact, cities do not grow and will not grow according to any plan, no matter how wise. Their growth is a necessary resultant of economic forces and economic accidents which nobody can foresee. . . .
>
> In every instance with which I am acquainted a zoning ordinance has become out of date within two or three years after its passage, sometimes generally out of date and sometimes sporadically out of date, with the result that the normal development of the territory has been artificially interfered with. People who rely upon the apparent stability of conditions established by zoning ordinances find themselves defeated in their expectations and in some of the cases of which I have knowledge the results are cruel.

Baker reiterated and expanded on these sentiments seven months later (July 10, 1926) in a letter to a lawyer in Chester, Pennsylvania:

> If a man puts a drug store in the wrong place, he soon learns it by finding that he has no patronage and moves to a new location with relatively little economic loss to the community. When the thing is attempted comprehensively, however, by one of these zoning ordinances, mistakes are far more burdensome and their correction more costly and difficult.

Four days later, in another letter to his Chester correspondent, Baker's antizoning rhetoric reached a new level, as he employed ideological arguments in his struggle against government overreaching:

If the right of private property is subject to the unrestrained caprice of village councils and the courts can do nothing more helpful than retire behind a conclusive presumption of soundness in legislative action, no matter how capricious or burdensome it appears on its face, then obviously we have outgrown the civilization established by the Constitution and have surrendered private ownership of property into a sort of communistic ownership and control upon which an entirely new order of both economic and social organizations will be based.

There is no evidence that Baker ever shared these political fears with the Court or in any public forum.

Baker's distaste for the social engineering flavor of this Progressive scheme was palpable in these words that appeared in a letter that Baker sent on May 25, 1926, to George T. Simpson. At the time he sent the letter, Baker was involved in another federal court zoning challenge, this time representing an orphanage against the Village of University Heights, which like Euclid was a suburb to the east of Cleveland:

It is difficult to illustrate to the court the extent to which some of these eccentric ordinances go. I have been in another case here in Ohio an instance in which a Jewish Orphanage Asylum, which is one of the best managed institutions of its kind in America, has been excluded from a village in which it owns a twenty-acre tract and in which it proposed to build a modern cottage-system orphanage.

According to Baker, when the matter of granting a building permit was referred to the "so-called zoning committee," that body rejected the idea "because they did not think it would be good for the village to have a large number of Jewish children in it." Baker told Simpson that if he were to relate that story to the court "it would be regarded as an improper effort to arouse religious prejudice and yet, of course, that is exactly the kind of misconduct we can expect from municipal authorities if they are given a free hand to indulge their prejudices and preferences." There was an undercurrent of anti-Semitism in several of the struggles to implement and defend zoning in metropolitan Cleveland, as pointed out by William Randle who reported that "'Jewish elements' [were] attacked in local publications for advancing apartment projects in the [Lakewood] area. The same tactics were used in East Cleveland." Of course, it would not be hard to find religious as well as racial restrictions in the covenants employed by the developers of many of the residential subdivisions being promoted in the Cleveland suburbs.

It would be easy to attribute Baker's legal representation of the forces opposed to zoning, which after all was a widely respected Progressive regulatory program, to a change in the former mayor's political stripes. In fact, Baker, whose supporters almost spoiled Franklin Roosevelt's nomination in 1932, would become an outspoken Democratic opponent of New Deal policies. It has also been suggested that as a hired legal gun Baker's politics and sympathies one way or the other were irrelevant. The letter to Simpson, indicated, however, that the struggle against zoning may have been consistent with Baker's long-seated distaste for religious prejudice and purveyors of ethnic bias. Perhaps that is why, according to Baker's biographer, Henry Ford attempted to prove that the Protestant-born Newton D. Baker (or was it Newman Becker?) was himself Jewish, as part of the automaker's shameful and virulent smear campaign against Jews.

As it turned out, Simpson was the only attorney to answer Baker's call for *amicus* support. While Baker in his oral argument disavowed an intention to discuss "abstract philosophy," Simpson was eager to enter the breach. The *amicus* brief was filed on behalf of three Minnesota corporations—the American Wood Products Company, the Northwestern Feed Company, and the Lyle Culvert & Road Equipment Company, along with one individual, T. Benson. A good deal of the discussion compared the zoning situation in the Twin Cities of Minneapolis–St. Paul with that in metropolitan Cleveland. All of these parties had a strong personal interest in the question of the legitimacy of zoning, as Simpson revealed when he noted that there was pending litigation in a federal court in Minnesota whose decision "will be influenced, and, perhaps, entirely controlled, by the opinion in the cause at bar." Simpson's prediction was right on target. In 1927, the trial court, after a reargument that followed the announcement of the holding in *Euclid v. Ambler*, dismissed the bill of complaint filed by Simpson's clients. The judge followed the deferential standard contained in the Supreme Court precedent, even though he felt that "the city [of Minneapolis] has dealt unjustly with these complainants," and the court of appeals affirmed two years later.

Simpson's rhetoric was a bit more strident and alarmist than Baker's. The *amicus* brief, for example, was designed "to aid the Court toward a more comprehensive view of the general situation which we believe confronts this Nation, growing out of the attempt by persons, not always actuated by unselfish motives, to import this principle of 'comprehensive zoning' into the affairs of its cities and villages." Simpson was particularly hard on officials in most American cities, noting that "the incompetency and dishonesty, which by reason of many factors, dominate their affairs, is known to all." He alleged that sometimes choice properties were "held by the members of the designating body, or their friends," while zoning restrictions were imposed "with the sole interest, and purpose, of driving the owners therefrom and to the property of the friends of the designating body." This passage would presage the allegations, and (much too often) actual examples, of corruption that plague zoning practices to this day.

Zoning itself, according to the Simpson brief, was an unwelcome and illegal immigrant, directly contrary to "*our* conception of property," which was the "*Anglo-Saxon* conception of the *right of the owner to own, use, and enjoy* his or her property." What Simpson called "blanket" or "comprehensive" zoning ordinances, in contrast, were "attempts to reverse the rule by which we American people have heretofore been guided, and [were], apparently, attempts to import into this country the European view that government is one of men and not of law." He warned that if "we forget the ideas which surrounded the original enactment of the Constitution of the United States, and follow after these theories, and strange gods, of Europe, we breed for the Nation trouble, and perhaps, disaster."

Simpson had explained to Baker that he had a specific target for his presentation: "In the preparation of the brief, I have had in mind not only my idea of the invasion of property rights by these zoning ordinances, but the fact that the brief will be scanned by [Minnesotan] Pierce Butler, who is personally familiar with the entire situation here in the Twin Cities." Butler and his right-thinking colleagues would, it was hoped, agree with the proposition that, "wherever it is situate, and by whomever zoning is imposed, *property is always 'taken' without compensation.*" On October 4, Chief Justice Taft announced that, upon Baker's motion, Simpson was formally granted leave to file his brief.

The second friend of the court brief would not be written or submitted at the behest, or with the apparent cooperation, of Baker's opposing counsel. Bettman's brief was filed with the permission of the Chief Justice on behalf of the National Conference on City Planning, the Ohio State Conference on City Planning, the National Housing Association, and the Massachusetts Federation of Town Planning Boards. The sole purpose of the brief was to discuss "the question of the constitutionality of comprehensive zoning," not "to argue any issues of either fact or law which may have been raised by the parties to the case, except as they relate" to the previous question. The brief resulted from the need to correct the appellee's use of "fallacious arguments on constitutional law, as well as entirely mistaken citation of authorities," along with the "many general expressions in the opinion of the District Judge [that] may be and are being interpreted as adverse to the validity of zoning." Also motivating the submission was the belief that zoning is "a vital necessity to the welfare of that increasing majority of the inhabitants of the United States who live in urban communities."

Bettman was not thinking about these issues for the first time. Far from it—he had been discussing and writing about many of the ideas discussed in the brief for years. For example, anyone who had reviewed his article on "The Constitutionality of Zoning," which appeared in the May 1924 issue of the *Harvard Law Review*, would have been quite familiar with many of the arguments that Bettman brought directly to the Court's attention in *Euclid v. Ambler*.

Bettman began his brief with a simple definition of what to some was apparently a confusing term: "Zoning is the regulation by districts of building development and uses of property." Like Metzenbaum, Bettman distinguished a "block" or "residential district" ordinance from zoning, which was more comprehensive in nature. And, like Metzenbaum, Bettman discussed the rapid spread of zoning, the situation in the Ohio courts, and the holding in the state courts of many other jurisdictions. In fact, there were only a few noticeable differences between the appellants' brief and that of its uninvited friends, or *amici*. But, to those fans of Bettman, particularly those from the planning profession, the differences helped determine the outcome of the case.

The first difference can be found in the short section labeled "This Court Has Sustained the Validity of Zoning Regulations." While Metzenbaum viewed *Euclid v. Ambler* as the first case in which the Supreme Court would consider a constitutional challenge to zoning, Bettman asserted that in two previous cases, *Welch v. Swazey* (1909) and *Hadacheck v. Sebastian* (1915), the Court "had occasion to pass upon the validity of ordinances of a zoning nature and in each case upheld the ordinance." The former case involved a Boston height limitation, while the latter concerned the exclusion from a "residential zone" of a brickyard and other industrial uses. The *Hadacheck* case was especially important because, to Bettman at least, it "effectively disposes of the contention of appellee that use regulation is unconstitutional though height and area regulation may not be." If the more primitive regulations in these two earlier cases passed constitutional muster, then comprehensive zoning would certainly be "emphatically more reasonable."

The second, more subtle, difference came with Bettman's assertion that "zoning is simply a modern mode or application to modern urban conditions of recognized and sanctioned methods of regulating property in the interest of the public health, convenience, safety, morals and welfare. Zoning bears distinct analogies to the recognized and sanctioned modes of such regulation." While Metzenbaum had also argued that as conditions became more complex, it became necessary to move beyond common-law nuisance, Bettman's analysis was more nuanced. Bettman reasoned, for example, that

> the law of nuisance operates by way of prevention as well as by suppression. The zoning ordinance, by segregating the industrial districts from the residential districts, aims to produce, by a process of prevention applied over the whole territory of the city

throughout an extensive period of time, the segregation of the noises and odors and turmoils necessarily incident to the operation of industry from those sections of the city in which the homes of the people are or may be appropriately located. The mode of regulation may be new; but the purpose and the fundamental justification are the same.

This was the first and most memorable of the "analogies" presented in Bettman's brief, the purpose of which was "to show that zoning represents no radically new type of property regulation, but merely a new application of sanctioned traditional methods for sanctioned traditional purposes. By grounding zoning in Supreme Court and common-law precedent, Bettman was making this new (and analogous) device easier for the less Progressive and reform-minded justices to digest.

By engaging in analogies, Bettman was not *equating* nuisance with zoning. Nor would he confine the police power to the suppression of nuisances: "the police power acts not only suppressively, but also constructively for the promotion of the general welfare." Again echoing Metzenbaum, Bettman emphasized that zoning was needed because of "the inadequacy of the technical law of nuisance to cope with the problems of contemporary municipal growth." The comprehensive, constructive approach taken by zoning made it not only more modern, but "more just, intelligent and reasonable" than its predecessors.

Third, Bettman confronted head-on Baker and Morgan's criticism that zoning was largely if not chiefly designed to achieve aesthetic purposes. "Zoning does aim to improve the good order of the cities," Bettman conceded, but that was "something quite different from the artistic or the beautiful." To illustrate his point, Bettman included a colorful comparison: "When we put the furnace in the cellar rather than in the living room, we are not actuated so much by dictates of good taste or aesthetic standards, as by the conviction that the living room will be a healthier place in which to live and the house a more generally healthful place." This would be true also of "the man who seeks to place the home for his children in an orderly neighborhood, with some open space and light and fresh air and quiet."

The final difference between Metzenbaum's and Bettman's approaches was found in that part of Bettman's brief that resembled most the approach taken in the famous "Brandeis Brief," which the future justice and Josephine Goldmark filed in support of maximum hours legislation for women in *Muller v. Oregon* (1908). Like Brandeis and Goldmark, Bettman complemented his traditional argument with extralegal information in order to bolster his assertion that "zoning is based upon a thorough and comprehensive study of the developments of modern American cities, with full consideration of economic factors of municipal growth, as well as the social factors." Bettman reported that "volumes have been written on the needs, the technique and methods with which these needs are met and the factors of the problem," although in the brief he had room "for only a short outline." This was not so much a difference in substance from Metzenbaum's attempts than a difference in style, emphasis, and use of sources for support.

A key component of Bettman's argument concerned the health advantages of home ownership and the threats that the modern commercial and industrial city posed to residential neighborhoods. He also took time to introduce expert analysis on the positive effect that zoning had on real estate values. Readers of the brief were provided with a three-page reading list of studies regarding the "relation of zoning to public health," "to public morals," "to public safety," and "to housing, living conditions, recreation, general welfare and prosperity." In the face of these findings, those claiming that zoning had no substantial relationship to these important governmental goals would carry a heavy burden of persuasion.

Amply supplied with a new and larger set of briefs, the Supreme Court heard the second oral argument in *Euclid v. Ambler* on Columbus Day, October 12, 1926. Metzenbaum's argument made a lasting, though not exactly positive, impression on at least one lawyer who was in attendance. Milton Handler, fresh out of Columbia's law school, was clerking for Justice Stone before embarking on a very long and distinguished career as a law professor at his alma mater, as a leading practitioner, and as a nationally recognized expert on antitrust law. More than sixty years after the event, in a letter to this author, Professor Handler recalled that he had thought in 1926 "that the Four Horsemen plus Taft would hold municipal zoning unconstitutional." He also remembered serving as a "Father Confessor" for Metzenbaum, who despite (or perhaps because of) this being his second appearance in the case was a "Nervous Nellie." The village's counsel was concerned that he had failed to wear a vest, because the chief justice had chastised "a western lawyer" who argued before the Court "dressed in cowboy clothes," informing the offender that he was in violation of Court rules. Metzenbaum was considering either returning to Cleveland for a vest or purchasing one in Washington. Handler advised him that his "five-button jacket with a military cut" would do the trick, but Metzenbaum "kept after [Handler] day and night, to be sure that my advice was correct."

The former clerk recalled as well that Metzenbaum's second and last oral argument before the Supreme Court was "quite a disaster." Most inappropriately, Metzenbaum "spent a substantial part of his limited time in denouncing the trial judge [Westenhaver] who had been a partner of Newton D. Baker and was appointed to the Court through Baker's assistance, then being Secretary of War in the Wilson cabinet," a tactic that Handler deemed "a total waste of time."

Handler contrasted the two attorneys in the zoning case in the following manner:

> I know that this [Metzenbaum's attack on Westenhaver] was poor advocacy and a waste of the limited time allotted to counsel for the presentation of his case. Baker was magnificent and, in my opinion, ranked with such extraordinary appellate counsel as John W. Davis, Charles Evans Hughes when at the bar, Wild Bill Donovan and others enjoying the fame that a skillful appellate advocate obtains through experience.

Nevertheless, Handler was pleased with the ultimate result, which he called a "welcome surprise." Looking back at the Taft Court, he observed that "it was very rare that Sutherland abandoned the others in the Four Horsemen group and it was even rarer for Taft to abandon his cohorts."

Readers of the *Cleveland Plain Dealer* encountered a decidedly less personal and colorful account of the second oral argument the day after the event, in an article headlined, "Nation Watches New Zoning Plea; Baker Reargues Euclid Case Which Involves Villages of Entire Country." According to this short article, Baker repeated that "his intention is not to demonstrate the general and comprehensive invalidity of all zoning ordinances, but that he holds a particular ordinance unconstitutional." Metzenbaum, again emphasizing the acceptance of the zoning concept by other courts, was quoted as asserting that seventeen states have "through their highest tribunals so firmly stamped their approval and validation, that the question of fundamental unconstitutionality has successfully been denied, literally, from coast to coast."

A couple of weeks after the Court rendered its judgment, in a letter dated December 6, 1926, Baker recalled what he had attempted to accomplish in his oral argument:

> I tried to develop a principle which could be applied in these cases by making the power of eminent domain the affirmative power and the police power the negative power and thus deducting a rule that whenever the public power was used merely to prevent a nuisance, it was the police power and could be exercised without compensation, but that whenever the public power was used to construct a public benefit, it was the power of eminent domain and could only be exercised upon compensation. I spent the whole summer trying to work out some distinction that would be philosophically sound.

Even today, lawyers, judges, and legal commentators struggle mightily with the distinction between the police power (the power to regulate) and the sovereign power of eminent domain (the power to take).

It appears from Baker's office file that at one time he and Morgan seriously considered filing a supplemental brief, but none was submitted. Metzenbaum, though, could not resist the temptation to make one last pitch to the justices; he filed a third brief. The overriding theme of this supplemental brief was that Ambler Realty carried a heavy burden of showing that the Euclid zoning ordinance, like all zoning ordinances, was "fundamentally" unconstitutional. This was not a debate about the reasonableness of the ordinance as applied to one landowner, although it appeared that in oral argument Baker was attempting to argue that the ordinance was unconstitutionally invalid "upon the ground of unreasonableness." (In support of this point, Metzenbaum inserted the quotation from the transcript of the first oral argument that he had secured from A. J. Hill.) Metzenbaum argued that Ambler Realty's failure to seek a zoning change or variance should be fatal to its claims.

Metzenbaum also provided an update on state court developments that had been handed down since the filing of his previous brief, along with a list of "unanswerable facts" raised by the record of the case as it was presented to the trial court. The most curious aspect of Metzenbaum's last word before the Court issued its ruling was his response to Bettman's *amici curiae* brief. Although Metzenbaum claimed that he was writing "with no intention of criticism and with a fitting respect for the brief," he apparently felt compelled to urge the Court not to allow "this brief, like its predecessor in the Trial Court below, to prejudice any of the rights of the Village." Metzenbaum was particularly troubled by "citations of so-called 'nuisance' and 'semi-nuisance' cases [such as *Hadacheck*] as supporting zoning ordinances." Apparently, Metzenbaum not only wanted a victory for his clients, but he wanted it on his own terms, for he believed strongly that the ordinance that he helped draft and that he was charged with defending could withstand Baker's assault *as is and on its own.*

Even after making his case in person two times and filing three formal briefs, Metzenbaum was still not prepared to rest. On November 1, he requested that the clerk of the Supreme Court distribute to the justices additional copies of either the 1913 or 1916 report of the New York Investigating Committee, " 'which really furnished the very basis and foundation for comprehensive zoning throughout the country.' " Metzenbaum was "particularly anxious that Justice Sutherland should have a copy of either the 1913 or the 1916 Report, because he did not hear the original argument of the case last January and in that argument I unfolded much that was contained in these Reports, whereas in the more recent argument I merely touched upon that subject and addressed myself more prominently in reference to the so-called 'facts' in the Record." The clerk's office complied with the request.

On November 14, the *New York Times* included an update on the still unresolved case: "Important Decision Expected on Zoning." The article reported that, given "widely differing State court decisions in New York, New Jersey and all over the country," and the fact that the nation's highest court was considering zoning's validity, "realty men in general are anxious for a full opinion defining the constitutional limitations of zoning for future guidance of cities and property owners." Those anticipating the Court's decision would have to be a little more patient, as the Court would not announce its decision for another eight days.

CHAPTER 6

Judgment Day

Beginning with its adjournment on November 1, 1926, the Supreme Court took a three-week break. In the early hours of November 21, the day before the justices reconvened, former Justice Joseph McKenna died at age 83. McKenna's retirement in January, 1925, had opened the seat that Justice Stone filled the following month. One can only speculate as to how Justice McKenna, who did not fit neatly into either the "Progressive" or "conservative" mold, would have responded to Ambler Realty's claims had he remained on the bench. Monday, November 22, was certainly not a normal "decision day" for the Court, which met for only two hours before recessing so that the justices could join President Calvin Coolidge and the other dignitaries at the funeral in the afternoon. Before closing the proceedings on that somber day, Taft said:

> No one who was present will forget the affecting scene and farewell in 1925, when the Justice in this room took his leave of the court and his colleagues. As a mark of love and a tribute of respect for his twenty-seven years of distinguished and useful service on this bench, the court will, after the delivery of opinions this morning, adjourn until Tuesday noon.

The justices then left to assume their new duties as honorary pallbearers.

During its brief Monday session, the Court delivered opinions in thirteen cases. Reviewing this baker's dozen as a set gives today's reader an important glimpse into the diverse nature of the Taft Court's caseload. Moreover, much like *Euclid* itself, the other representative decisions addressed some of the important legal issues of the day and demonstrated the sometimes profound splits on the Court in the 1920s.

No fewer than three of the Court's decisions for November 22 involved prohibition. *United States v. One Ford Coupe Automobile* involved the seizure of a rum-running vehicle. The majority, in an opinion written by Justice Brandeis, answered "yes" to the question of "whether an automobile, which was seized by a prohibition agent, may be forfeited under [a federal statute] if it was being used for the purpose of depositing or concealing tax-unpaid illicit liquors with the intent to defraud the United States of the taxes imposed thereon," even if the owner of the vehicle claimed to have no knowledge that it was being used for illegal purposes. Three dissenting justices— Butler, joined by McReynolds and Sutherland—insisted that the pre-Prohibition taxes on beverage liquors (and their harsh forfeiture provisions) were no longer in effect.

In a second forfeiture case, *Van Oster v. Kansas*, Justice Stone wrote for a unanimous court in rejecting the pleas of another allegedly innocent vehicle owner. In this instance, the owner challenged a Kansas confiscation law that went farther than the National Prohibition Act.

The misstep of a trial judge in a federal district court in California led to reversal of the convictions of defendants charged with conspiring to possess and transport intoxicating liquors in the third prohibition case of the day. After the jury had failed to come to agreement following several hours of deliberations, the judge inquired as to the numerical split among the jurors; the foreman responded, without indicating which side had the majority, that the vote stood at nine to three. The Supreme Court, in *Brasfield v. United States*, resolved a split among the federal circuit courts by concluding, "We deem it essential to the fair and impartial conduct of the trial, that the [judge's] inquiry itself should be regarded as ground for reversal." For those keeping score on November 22, 1926, it was government 2, moonshiners and rum-runners 1.

In another criminal law case that day, *Hudson v. United States*, the Court rejected the assertion that a court could not impose a prison sentence on a defendant who had entered a plea of *nolo contendere*, in which the accused person fails to contest the charges without technically entering a guilty plea. Because one federal circuit had issued opinions in support of the notion that "the plea in effect is conditioned upon the imposition of a lighter penalty," the Supreme Court decided to hear the case. Justice Stone, for a unanimous court, engaged in a detailed analysis of English sources from the eighteenth and nineteenth century, concluding that the "historical background is too meager and inconclusive to be persuasive." This case demonstrated that, even after 150 years of political independence, the Supreme Court maintained the Anglo-American legal chain.

Euclid v. Ambler was one of two property rights cases decided on November 22; in both cases Justice Sutherland wrote the Court's opinion. The nonzoning case involved a long-standing dispute between the United States government and the Yankton Sioux Tribe of South Dakota over the ownership and use of the Red Pipestone Quarries in southwestern Minnesota. From this sacred site, the Yankton and other Native Americans have long extracted the soft, red stone that was used to shape the peace pipe (calumet). The Court in 1926 was interpreting the intent and implications of an 1858 treaty by which the tribe ceded some lands to the federal government but received the government's assurance that the tribe would continue to possess "free and unrestricted use of the Red Pipe-stone quarry." By the time the dispute over ownership and use of the quarries reached the High Court, members of Congress, government and tribal officials, and lower court judges had all wrestled with the questions of the nature of the tribe's interest, the effects of non-Indian settlement in the sacred area, and the value of the disputed lands.

In its 1926 decision in *Yankton Sioux Tribe v. United States*, the Supreme Court disagreed with the lower court's determination that the tribe owned only an easement, that is, a right in, but not title to, the lands. However, developments on the ground made it "impossible" in the Court's opinion to "restore the Indians to their former rights because the lands have been opened to settlement and large portions of them are now in the possession of innumerable innocent purchasers." As a second-best alternative, the Court concluded that, because the tribe had legal title to the site, it was "entitled to just compensation as for a taking under the power of eminent domain." In other words, because the federal government had in effect "taken" the land from the Yankton, the way it did when it exercised its sovereign power to condemn property needed for a public use or purpose, the United States would now, after the fact, be required to pay to the tribe in damages the value of the land. A similar argument—that the Village of Euclid had in effect "taken" the property of Ambler Realty Company—was, in effect, rejected that same day in another Sutherland opinion. Two years later, the tribe did cede their rights to the government, in exchange for a payment of over $330,000 (which included interest and legal fees). In 1937, the government designated the area Pipestone National Monument, reserving to Native Americans the right to quarry.

Much of the Court's work product that fall Monday involved consideration of the legitimacy of regulations affecting business and industry. Beginning in the late nineteenth century, picking up steam during the Progressive Era that led up to the nation's involvement in World War I, and continuing even during the postwar, conservative "return to normalcy," federal, state, and local lawmakers had enacted a wide range of social and economic controls. In addition to zoning, the regulatory fare on November 22 included professional licensing, public utility rate-setting, trust-busting, and controls on common carriers. This was the area of the Court's workload that exerted the most pressure on the chief justice's efforts to speak with a unified voice by eliminating dissents.

The Court gave short shrift to an argument brought by a disgruntled plaintiff who challenged Minnesota's legislative requirement that licensed dentists must first obtain a diploma from an accredited dental college. The unsuccessful applicant urged the Court to recognize that the diploma requirement "is unreasonable, arbitrary and discriminatory, and violates the due process clause and other provisions of the Fourteenth Amendment." In *Graves v. Minnesota*, all of the justices joined Justice Sanford's opinion in support of the state's regulatory power. The Court observed that the state legislature's determination that the diploma requirement helped "to safeguard properly the public health . . . must be given great weight." Indeed, the highly deferential opinion emphasized that "every presumption is to be indulged in favor of the validity of the statute," particularly "in the light of the principle that the State is primarily the judge of regulations required in the interest of public safety and welfare, and its police statutes may only be declared unconstitutional where they are arbitrary or unreasonable attempts to exercise the authority vested in it in the public interest." Perhaps Taft's influence was felt by Justices Butler, McReynolds, and Van Devanter, who officially kept silent despite the extreme respect the decision accorded state regulators who arguably violated Fourteenth Amendment rights.

Unanimity was maintained in three other decisions, all of which were losses for business and industry. The first case involved an unsuccessful effort by the Southern Pacific Company to recover additional charges from the government for the transportation on the company's railroad of "military impendimenta" (that is, baggage and equipment) for the War Department in 1916 and 1917. The court of claims rejected the company's claim for additional charges tied to a special, enhanced tariff that the company had on file with the Interstate Commerce Commission (ICC). There was no express agreement by the government to pay the additional charges or even any proof that government regulators were aware of the extra tariff. In *Southern Pacific Co. v. United States*, the Supreme Court, in an opinion by Justice Stone, affirmed the trial court's assessment.

The second business regulation case was also a loss for a railroad, this time the New York Central, the company from which the Van Sweringen brothers had purchased the Nickel Plate Road. In *United States v. New York Central Railroad Co.*, Justice Stone, writing for eight justices (Sutherland did not participate), supported the ICC, which had ruled in favor of the state of New York in the state's dispute with the railroad. At the state's urging the ICC issued an order compelling the railroad "to provide transportation service between the public terminal of the Erie Barge Canal at Buffalo [owned by the state] and shippers located along its tracks and along the lines of other railroads with which it can interchange traffic." The railroad made a federal case out of its dispute with the state, and a federal district court issued an order blocking the ICC's order. The lower court based its order on the belief that the federal statute did not grant the ICC the power to hear a claim brought by the state, which was the owner of a facility and not an interstate carrier. This order was reversed by the Supreme Court, which held that "a state, when its interests are concerned, as well as a private individual, whether carrier or not, may file a complaint with the commission." The justices were not troubled by the fact that the transportation issue before the Court seemed to be confined to one state. Justice Stone wrote, "Where, as here, interstate and intrastate transactions are interwoven, the regulation of the latter is so incidental to and inseparable from the regulation of the former as properly to be deemed included in the authority over interstate commerce conferred by statute." This decision was just a preview of the expansion of congressional power to regulate commerce that would take place over the following few decades.

In the third decision in this group, *Anderson v. Shipowners Association of the Pacific Coast*, the Court reversed the summary dismissal of a claim brought by a member of the Seaman's Union of America against an association of ship owners on the Pacific coast. According to the plaintiff, the members of the association violated the federal Anti-Trust Act when they "entered into a combination to control the employment, upon such vessels, of all seamen upon the Pacific Coast." Justice Sutherland, speaking for all of his brethren, held that, "taking the allegations of the bill at their face value, as we must do in the absence of countervailing facts or explanations," the plaintiff had, in fact, presented enough allegations to warrant a remand to the trial court for further proceedings. That was the extent of the Supreme Court's holding — the seaman was entitled to his day in court. As it turned out, once those proceedings occurred, the trial court and the court of appeals agreed that no statutory violation had actually occurred.

The fissures on the Court were more evident in another business regulation case, this one involving the rates set by the Public Service Commission of Indiana. A federal district court had questioned the validity of the rates set by the commission for the Indianapolis Water Company. The commission agreed with the company that its current rates were too low. However, the company and the commission parted ways when it came to deciding on the extent of the rate raise. The trial court challenged the valuation figures used by the commission in setting the new rate and concluded that the commission had erred by underassessing the present value of the company's assets. This valuation was crucial to the rate-setting function, as the commission set the rates at a level that assured the company an adequate level of return on its overall investment. The company charged that the rates were confiscatory, given that the commission (in the company's view) had underestimated the value of the assets by at least a few million dollars. The trial court sided with the company, and the Supreme Court agreed, in an opinion for six justices written by Justice Butler. The majority, looking over the shoulder of the expert-based commission findings, concluded that,

> in determining present value, consideration must be given to prices and wages prevailing at the time of the investigation; and, in the light of all the circumstances, there must be an honest and intelligent forecast as to probable price and wage levels during a reasonable period in the immediate future. In every confiscation case, the future as well as the present must be regarded. It must be determined whether the rates complained of are yielding and will yield, over and above the amounts required to pay taxes and proper operating charges, a sum sufficient to constitute just compensation for the use of the property employed to furnish the service; that is, a reasonable rate of return on the value of the property at the time of the investigation and for a reasonable time in the immediate future.

If the *Euclid* majority had engaged in the same detailed mathematical recalculations that Justice Butler produced in *McCardle v. Indianapolis Water Co.*, calculations that indulged in the property owner's presumptions regarding value and the reasonableness of a rate of return, it is highly probable that he and the two other *Euclid* dissenters would have found themselves on the winning side.

As it turned out, the three least conservative members of the Taft Court at the time did not concur with Butler's rationale. Justice Holmes concurred only in the result, while Justice Brandeis, joined by Justice Stone, dissented. The dissenters challenged the district court's use of a "spot" reproduction cost method to assess the value of the company's assets. In other words, the lower court, in reversing the commission's findings, asked what it would cost if the power plant and other company facilities could be built *instantly* at today's prices. Brandeis was incredulous: "'Spot' reproduction would be impossible of accomplishment without the aid of Aladdin's lamp. . . . The search for value can hardly be aided by a hypothetical estimate of the cost of replacing the plant at a particular moment, when actual reproduction would require a period that must be measured by years." Moreover, the two dissenters emphasized that the facts before the Court did "not justify holding that rates which yield a return of less than 7 per cent. would be so unreasonably low as to be confiscatory." Confiscation, it would appear, was in the eye of the beholder.

The other decisions announced on November 22 included the issuance of a final order in a boundary dispute between Michigan and Wisconsin, a case in which the Supreme Court exercised its original, as opposed to appellate, jurisdiction (*Michigan v. Wisconsin*); and the rejection of a patent infringement case brought by the manufacturer of rubber shoe heels (*I. T. S. Rubber Co. v. Essex Rubber Co.*). Both of these decisions were unanimous.

Looking back from the vantage point of the early twenty-first century, there is no question that *Euclid v. Ambler* was the most memorable of the ample number of decisions handed down on the morning of Justice McKenna's funeral. And, at least since the time that federal prohibition was lifted in the 1930s, the zoning decision announced on November 22, 1926, has had the greatest impact on the lives of Americans from coast to coast and in between. Justice Sutherland wrote for a majority of six, as Justices Van Devanter, McReynolds, and Butler dissented without opinion. While Sutherland's opinion in *Euclid v. Ambler* was not formally divided into sections, the discussion fell into five discrete parts. Beginning with a detailed explication of the crucial facts regarding the zoning ordinance and its effect on Ambler Realty's parcel, the opinion moved to a summary of the goals and procedural roadmap of the landowner's lawsuit. The Court's analysis in the crucial third section sought to reconcile the permanence of constitutional principles with the rapidly changing conditions of the modern world. The two closing parts of *Euclid v. Ambler* addressed the crux of the dispute — the protection of residential neighborhoods — and described just what the Court had and had not resolved in this one, important opinion.

Foundational Fact-Finding

Because *Euclid v. Ambler* was essentially a real estate dispute, the opinion logically began with a description of the parcel in its geographic and legal context. The reader learned in the first sentence that the village "is an Ohio municipal corporation" and in the second that the village "adjoins and practically is a suburb of Cleveland." The order in which these two facts were presented provided an important clue as to the outcome of the decision, for Justice Sutherland emphasized the legally independent status of Euclid before describing its "practical" status as a suburb. Curiously, at times the opinion eschewed exactness, noting, for example, that the village had an "estimated population" of five to ten thousand and an area of "from 12 to 14 square miles." The opinion described the village's major thoroughfares and railroad lines and then homed in on the exact location of Ambler Realty's 68 acres.

Probably because zoning was still a relatively new and unfamiliar concept, Justice Sutherland devoted several paragraphs to a detailed description of the particular features of Euclid's 1922 zoning ordinance. He listed the permitted uses in all six use districts and described the height limits in all three height districts by feet and stories, and the minimum square footage requirements in all four area districts.

Applying the zoning ordinance to the specific parcel yielded the following description:

> Appellee's tract of land comes under U-2, U-3 and U-6. The first strip of 620 feet immediately north of Euclid Avenue falls in class U-2, the next 130 feet to the north, in U-3, and the remainder in U-6. The uses of the first 620 feet, therefore, do not include apartment houses, hotels, churches, schools, or other public and semipublic buildings, or other uses enumerated in respect of U-3 to U-6, inclusive. The uses of the next 130 feet include all of these, but exclude industries, theatres, banks, shops, and the various other uses set forth in respect of U-4 to U-6, inclusive.

In a footnote, Sutherland explained that this description varied from that provided by federal district judge Westenhaver, who "seemed to think that the frontage of this property on Euclid Avenue to a depth of 150 feet came under U-1 district and was available only for single family dwellings." This difference might have made a significant difference in the economic impact of the regulation on the value of the parcel, but ultimately the question of value did not affect the outcome of the case.

The final paragraph of the opening section of the opinion reviewed the way in which the zoning ordinance was administered and enforced. Justice Sutherland pointed out that procedures were in place for relieving the burdens on those landowners who suffered special burdens under the zoning regime: "Decisions of the inspector of buildings may be appealed to the board [of zoning appeals] by any person claiming to be adversely affected by any such decision. The board is given power in specific cases of practical difficulty or unnecessary hardship to interpret the ordinance in harmony with its general purpose and intent, so that the public health, safety and general welfare may be secure and substantial justice done." In this way, the majority made clear that some flexibility was built into what might otherwise appear to have been a set of rigid restrictions.

The Lawsuit Explained

In the second portion of the opinion, Justice Sutherland turned to Ambler Realty's specific legal challenge, noting,

> The ordinance is assailed on the grounds that it is in derogation of § 1 of the Fourteenth Amendment to the Federal Constitution in that it deprives appellee of liberty and property without due process of law and denies it the equal protection of the law, and that it offends against certain provisions of the Constitution of the State of Ohio. The prayer of the bill is for an injunction restraining the enforcement of the ordinance and all attempts to impose or maintain as to appellee's property any of the restrictions, limitations or conditions.

There were two essential elements included in the language quoted above. First, Ambler Realty's challenge was solely on constitutional grounds. The landowner was not alleging, for example, that the village has exceeded the authority granted under the state legislation authorizing local governments to engage in zoning. Second, Ambler Realty asked the Supreme Court to find that the mere enactment of the zoning ordinance was so inherently unconstitutional that the village must be prevented from enforcing its provisions.

The opinion then included Ambler Realty's specific assertions regarding the allegedly confiscatory effects of the passage of the zoning ordinance. It was evident that the landowner was not prevented from continuing to use improved land, but that Ambler Realty had instead speculated on the future value of the undeveloped parcel: "The bill alleges that the tract of land has been held for years for the purpose of selling and developing it for industrial uses, for which it was specifically adapted, being immediately in the path of progressive industrial development." Moreover, Sutherland pointed out that Ambler Realty had averred "that prospective [not currently identifiable] buyers of land for industrial, commercial, and residential uses in the metropolitan district of Cleveland are deterred from buying any part of this land because of the existence of the zoning ordinance" and that there was a resulting need to litigate in order "to vindicate the right to use the land for lawful and legitimate purposes."

The Court then presented, without comment or correction from Metzenbaum's briefs, Ambler Realty's version of the financial loss it would suffer should the justices uphold the zoning ordinance:

> For such [industrial] uses it has a market value of about $10,000 per acre, but if the use be limited to residential purposes the market value is not in excess of $2,500 per acre; that the first 200 feet of the parcel back from Euclid Avenue, if unrestricted in respect of use, has a value of $150 per front foot, but if limited to residential uses, and ordinary mercantile business be excluded therefrom, its value is not in excess of $50 per front foot.

An important point overlooked by many subsequent commentators, litigators, and judges is that the Court in *Euclid v. Ambler* did not say that these figures were necessarily accurate. Instead, the Court established that, even if Ambler Realty's estimate had been correct, something Metzenbaum was never willing to concede, its constitutional rights had not been violated. In other words, this was more in the nature of an acceptable worst-case scenario than the endorsement of the landowner's calculation.

There is further evidence that the lawsuit before the Court was a direct assault on the zoning ordinance upon its enactment, what in modern terminology is deemed a "facial challenge": Sutherland agreed with Judge Westenhaver that, Metzenbaum's argument to the contrary, Ambler Realty's suit was not premature, even though the landowner "had made no effort to obtain a building permit or apply to the zoning board of appeals for relief, as it might have done under the terms of the ordinance." But this preliminary victory ultimately spelled defeat for Ambler Realty, which now carried the heavy burden of proving its serious allegation "that the ordinance of its own force operates greatly to reduce the value of appellee's lands and destroy their marketability for industrial, commercial and residential uses." By directing their "attack . . . against the ordinance as an entirety," the landowner was asking the Court to question and ultimately negate a legislative decision by local elected officials. Would the Court agree with Ambler Realty's assertion that "the existence and maintenance of the ordinance in effect constitutes a present invasion of appellee's property rights and a threat to continue it"?

Changing Conditions and Constant Meanings

Before moving to a traditional analysis of common law concepts and zoning decisions from state courts, Sutherland followed the example in Metzenbaum's brief by considering the changing and increasingly complex urban social conditions that gave rise to modern land-use regulatory techniques:

> Building zone laws are of modern origin. They began in this country about twenty-five years ago. Until recent years, urban life was comparatively simple; but with the great increase and concentration of population, problems have developed, and constantly are developing, which require, and will continue to require, additional restrictions in respect of the use and occupation of private lands in urban communities. Regulations, the wisdom, neces-

sity and validity of which, as applied to existing conditions, are so apparent that they are now uniformly sustained, a century ago, or even half a century ago, probably would have been rejected as arbitrary and oppressive. Such regulations are sustained, under the complex conditions of our day, for reasons analogous to those which justify traffic regulations, which, before the advent of automobiles and rapid transit street railways, would have been condemned as fatally arbitrary and unreasonable.

The Court did not blind itself to the fact that, despite several notable cases in which modern reforms such as maximum work hours had been struck down, in the overwhelming majority of cases since the turn of the twentieth century, the justices had upheld legislative reforms that had been challenged as confiscatory and arbitrary. This was especially true in the area of prezoning, land-use regulation, which, as noted in Chapter 3, was rarely invalidated by a Court that otherwise prided itself on protecting property and contract rights.

To those who might question the Court's commitment to eternal constitutional truths, Sutherland pointed out that, "while the meaning of constitutional guaranties never varies, the scope of their application must expand or contract to meet the new and different conditions which are constantly coming within the field of their operation." He continued his depiction of an organic, adaptable Constitution, literally emphasizing a crucial distinction: "But although a degree of elasticity is thus imparted, not to the *meaning*, but to the *application* of constitutional principles, statutes and ordinances, which, after giving due weight to the new conditions, are found clearly not to conform to the Constitution, of course, must fall."

Sutherland then turned to the "police power," a term that appears nowhere in the text of the Constitution but that is the foundation for a wide body of government restrictions passed in furtherance of the "general welfare," a phrase that of course appears in the Preamble. There was no bright line separating "legitimate from illegitimate assumption of power." Once again, "circumstances and conditions" were key: "A regulatory zoning ordinance, which would be clearly valid as applied to the great cities, might be clearly invalid as applied to rural communities." This time following the *amicus* Bettman's lead, Sutherland turned to the common law of nuisance: "In solving doubts, the maxim *sic utere tuo ut alienum non laedas* [roughly translated as "use your property so as not to injure that of another"], which lies at the foundation of so much of the common law of nuisances, ordinarily will furnish a fairly helpful clew. And the law of nuisances, likewise, may be consulted, not for the purpose of controlling, but for the helpful aid of its analogies in the process of ascertaining the scope of, the power." This last point was important, for Sutherland refused to hamstring the police power by limiting it solely to the elimination or avoidance of nuisance.

Nuisance was to be a guide, an exemplar, but not a litmus test for legality. Once again, the specific circumstances were key. "Thus," Sutherland wrote, "the question whether the power exists to forbid the erection of a building of a particular kind or for a particular use, like the question whether a particular thing is a nuisance, is to be determined, not by an abstract consideration of the building or of the thing considered apart, but by considering it in connection with the circumstances and the locality." In the following sentence, Sutherland changed Bettman's metaphor (a furnace in the living room) to this memorable version: "A nuisance may be merely a right thing in the wrong place, — like a pig in the parlor instead of the barnyard." Sutherland then articulated a highly deferential position for the judicial review of local zoning decisions: "If the validity of the legislative classification for zoning purposes be fairly debatable, the legislative judgment must be allowed to control." For the next eighty-plus years, landowners challenging local land-use restrictions would be frustrated by this lax standard.

Like Metzenbaum, Sutherland then reviewed those prezoning restrictions that had already passed judicial muster, such as height restrictions, building codes, and the exclusion of offensive, nuisance-like activities from residential areas. The majority anticipated a fairness-based objection to the fact that zoning excludes all industrial uses, offensive and inoffensive alike, from residential sections: "The inclusion of a reasonable margin, to insure effective enforcement, will not put a stamp upon a law, otherwise valid, the stamp of invalidity." Government classifications that are neither unreasonable nor arbitrary will pass the test.

In a paragraph loaded with serious implications for local government regulation in and well beyond the area of land use, Sutherland rejected Baker's assertion that "a mere suburb of the City of Cleveland" did not have the power to divert the inexorable flow of industrial development from the central city. Size did not matter, legal status did:

> But the village, though physically a suburb of Cleveland, is politically a separate municipality, with powers of its own and authority to govern itself as it sees fit within the limits of the organic law of its creation and the State and Federal Constitutions. Its governing authorities, presumably representing a majority of its inhabitants and voicing their will, have determined, not that industrial development shall cease at its boundaries, but that the course of such development shall proceed within definitely fixed lines.

The state of Ohio's decision to authorize each municipality, even small suburban ones such as Euclid, to engage in zoning in order to protect the parochial interest of its own citizens would be respected by the Taft Court. In the same fashion, justices in the 1970s would refuse to order school buses to cross seemingly artificial school district boundaries in order to accomplish metropolitan-wide desegregation.

The *Euclid v. Ambler* Court did open the door to a possible challenge should one municipality's selfishness cause widespread harm: "It is not meant by this, however, to exclude the possibility of cases where the general public interest would so far outweigh the interest of the municipality that the municipality would not be allowed to stand in the way." Despite this warning, however, the overwhelming legacy of the case has been local independence, not regional cooperation.

The Crux of the Matter

There was an ample and long line of precedent for the practice of excluding industry from residential districts. Such was not the case for zoning's segregation of businesses and apartments from detached dwellings. Therefore, the question facing the U.S. Supreme Court for the first time "involves the validity of what is really the crux of the more recent zoning legislation, namely, the creation and maintenance of residential districts, from which business and trade of every sort, including hotels and apartment houses, are excluded."

Fortunately, Sutherland, guided by Metzenbaum and Bettman, had at his disposal "numerous and conflicting" state court decisions on the topic. In reviewing that decisional database, the majority perceived a trend: "those which broadly sustain the power greatly outnumber those which deny altogether or narrowly limit it; and it is very apparent that there is a constantly increasing tendency in the direction of the broader view." Included in the "broader" group were case citations from Massachusetts, Louisiana, New York, Illinois, Minnesota, Wisconsin, Kansas, California, and Rhode Island; on the other side stood a curious trio—Maryland, New Jersey, and Texas. Moreover, some of the states with unfriendly decisions had more recently moved into the prozoning group.

The courts in the larger group of cases "agree[d] that the exclusion of buildings devoted to business, trade, etc., from residential districts, bears a rational relation to the health and safety of the community." The choice of the adjective "rational" was important, as the state courts that approved zoning did not require a "necessary" or "essential" connection between the means of zoning and health and safety ends such as the protection of children from injury, fire protection, and traffic regulation and maintenance. Following this compendium of case citations, Sutherland included generous quotations from two cases upholding zoning—one from Illinois, the other from Louisiana.

From legal experts, Sutherland turned to other professionals who lined up in support of height, area, and use regulation. Metzenbaum had emphasized that experts from many fields were responsible for the development and spread of zoning, and he had been anxious to get into the justices' hands examples of their handiwork. Apparently, Euclid counsel's perseverance, augmented by Bettman's skillful (and Brandeisian) brief, had paid off. Sutherland noted,

> The matter of zoning has received much attention at the hands of commissions and experts, and the results of their investigations have been set forth in comprehensive reports. These reports, which bear every evidence of painstaking consideration, concur in

the view that the segregation of residential, business, and industrial buildings will make it easier to provide fire apparatus suitable for the character and intensity of the development in each section; that it will increase the safety and security of home life; greatly tend to prevent street accidents, especially to children, by reducing the traffic and resulting confusion in residential sections; decrease noise and other conditions which produce or intensify nervous disorders; preserve a more favorable environment in which to rear children, etc.

The experts focused special attention on the phenomenon of "the coming of the apartment houses," which would slow down "the development of detached house sections." The future of the American bedroom community, dominated by single-family detached dwellings, was greatly enhanced by the majority's acceptance of the experts' view that "in such sections very often the apartment house is a mere parasite, constructed in order to take advantage of the open spaces and attractive surroundings created by the residential character of the district." Moreover, as more apartment houses are built, they block sunlight and fresh air, increase noise, crowd the streets, and "depriv[e] children of the privilege of quiet and open spaces for play, enjoyed by those in more favored localities." When apartment houses are located in the wrong environment, they "come very close to being nuisances," Sutherland noted, returning to Bettman's primary theme. The message of this section of the opinion was clear: should the justices find zoning to be within the acceptable range of the police power, they, unlike Moses Cleaveland, would not be entering uncharted territory.

"A Gradual Approach"

Given the rapid growth of zoning in the 1920s, supported by certain real estate interests, reformers, and state and federal officials, Sutherland and his colleagues would have strong reason to believe that Ambler Realty's challenge would not be the last of its kind. In the final section of the opinion, the majority set the ground rules for future challenges not only to zoning but to a wide range of government regulatory programs that would arguably have a negative impact on private property rights and values.

First, the Court reiterated its position that local governments would be given a strong benefit of the doubt:

> If these reasons, thus summarized, do not demonstrate the wisdom or sound policy in all respects of those restrictions which we have indicated as pertinent to the inquiry, at least, the reasons are sufficiently cogent to preclude us from saying, as it must be said before the ordinance can be declared unconstitutional, that such provisions are clearly arbitrary and unreasonable, having no substantial relation to the public health, safety, morals, or general welfare.

It was evident from the sentence quoted above, which amounted to the holding of the case, that Metzenbaum had countered Baker's effort in the first oral argument to convert the lawsuit from a facial attack on the constitutionality of "Zoning and District ordinances" into an "as applied" challenge based upon the specific ordinance's "application to the particular parcel belonging to the Complainant." There was vindication, too, for Bettman, who had convinced skeptical proponents of planning and zoning that it was important to frame a brief that was "designed to discuss solely the question of the constitutionality of comprehensive zoning." Baker's gambit had not worked.

The Court in *Ambler v. Realty* did leave the door open to upholding challenges to zoning, in which provisions of specific ordinances would be "concretely applied to particular premises . . . or to particular conditions, or to be considered in connection with specific complaints," so long as the landowner carried its burden by meeting the demanding "clearly arbitrary or unreasonable" standard. In the case before the Court, however, Ambler Realty had brought an unsuccessful attempt based "upon the broad ground that the mere existence and threatened enforcement of the ordinance, by materially and adversely affecting values and curtailing the opportunities of the market, constitute a present and irreparable injury." The Court would not grant an injunction against the enforcement of the restrictions found in the zoning ordinance based on the allegation that Ambler

Realty could not sell some portion of its parcel "for certain enumerated uses because of the general and broad restraints of the ordinance."

The majority was confident that the Court's prudence, its refusal to speculate as to particular injuries to Ambler Realty in the future, was warranted in this instance. "In the realm of constitutional law, especially," Sutherland observed, "this court has perceived the embarrassment which is likely to result from an attempt to formulate rules or decide questions beyond the necessities of the immediate issue." In contrast, the Court "has preferred to follow the method of a gradual approach to the general by a systematically guarded application and extension of constitutional principles to particular cases as they arise, rather than by out of hand attempts to establish general rules to which future cases must be fitted." This was particularly true, he noted, in cases involving "questions arising under the due process clause of the Constitution as applied to the exercise of the flexible powers of police." On the vote of six justices, Judge Westenhaver's decision favoring Ambler Realty was reversed.

George Sutherland had been on the Supreme Court for a little over four years when Chief Justice Taft announced the holding in *Euclid v. Ambler*. He would remain on the Court until January 17, 1938, when, following Justice Van Devanter's departure on June 2, 1937, Sutherland vacated his seat. Several weeks before Sutherland's departure, on March 9, 1937, President Franklin Delano Roosevelt had introduced to the American people in one of his memorable fireside chats his "Court-Packing Plan." The plan, which never came to fruition, was designed to inject "new and younger" (and more sympathetic) blood into the judicial system. The president, who was frustrated by conservative Supreme Court decisions finding unconstitutional key New Deal programs, explained, "Whenever a Judge or Justice of any Federal Court has reached the age of seventy and does not avail himself of the opportunity to retire on a pension, a new member shall be appointed by the President then in office, with the approval, as required by the Constitution, of the Senate of the United States." Historians continue to debate whether Roosevelt's court-packing plan resulted in a switch in attitudes more favorable to New Deal reforms, or whether the Court was already undergoing internal changes unaffected by these external stimuli. In any event,

January 17, 1938, marked the end of Sutherland's long and notable record of public service. He would die four years later.

Sutherland's opinion in *Euclid v. Ambler*, and indeed his entire career before and during his years on the High Court, indicate that simplistic labels such as "conservative," "reactionary," "progressive," and "liberal" mask the complexity of the judicial decision-making process and the fluid, as opposed to rigid and static, nature of judicial philosophies. By reviewing some of the highlights of Sutherland's judicial career, we can gain a richer understanding of his landmark 1926 opinion.

To some, Sutherland will always be associated with his opinions for the Court in two decisions that were an anathema to those on the political left: *Adkins v. Children's Hospital* in 1923 and *Carter v. Carter Coal Co.* in 1936. In *Adkins*, the Court struck down a 1918 act of Congress "providing for the fixing of minimum wages for women and children in the District of Columbia." Citing some of the most controversial precedents of the early twentieth century, Sutherland noted, "That the right to contract about one's affairs is a part of the liberty of the individual protected by this clause [the Due Process Clause of the Fourteenth Amendment], is settled by the decisions of this Court and is no longer open to question." This freedom of contract, while not absolute, was strongly protected by the Constitution, and Sutherland could find no precedent to support a departure from the holding in *Lochner v. New York*, the 1905 case invalidating a statute creating a ten-hour work day for bakers. Indeed, the *Adkins* opinion quoted generously from Justice Rufus Peckham's opinion in *Lochner*, the bête noire of Progressive reformers who sought to use legislation to improve the wages and working conditions of working-class Americans.

Despite his palpable distaste for the legislation before the Court, Sutherland eschewed an absolutist stand in *Adkins*. Instead, he noted that the Court's difficult function was to draw the line between the individual's right and the public good:

> It has been said that legislation of the kind now under review is required in the interest of social justice, for whose ends freedom of contract may lawfully be subjected to restraint. The liberty of the individual to do as he pleases, even in innocent matters, is not

absolute. It must frequently yield to the common good, and the line beyond which the power of interference may not be pressed is neither definite nor unalterable but may be made to move, within limits not well defined, with changing need and circumstance. Any attempt to fix a rigid boundary would be unwise as well as futile. But, nevertheless, there are limits to the power, and when these have been passed, it becomes the plain duty of the courts in the proper exercise of their authority to so declare. To sustain the individual freedom of action contemplated by the Constitution, is not to strike down the common good but to exalt it; for surely the good of society as a whole cannot be better served than by the preservation against arbitrary restraint of the liberties of its constituent members.

Sutherland would revisit these themes—line drawing, the common good, and judicial vigilance against arbitrary government action—in the *Euclid v. Ambler* opinion.

More than a dozen years after *Adkins*, in *Carter Coal*, Sutherland once again found that Congress had exceeded its constitutional reach, this time in enacting the Bituminous Coal Conservation Act of 1935. This comprehensive regulatory scheme was designed to reinstate many of the National Recovery Administration (NRA) controls for the coal industry in the wake of the Court's anti-NRA decision in 1935, *Schechter Poultry Corp. v. United States*. Congressional reliance on the power to regulate interstate commerce was misplaced in this setting:

> The effect of the labor provisions of the act, including those in respect of minimum wages, wage agreements, collective bargaining, and the Labor Board and its powers, primarily falls upon production and not upon commerce; and confirms the further resulting conclusion that production is a purely local activity. It follows that none of these essential antecedents of production constitutes a transaction in or forms any part of interstate commerce.

Within a few years, the Court would reject this narrow interpretation of "commerce," much to the consternation of conservative critics then and now.

To Sutherland, these labor issues were not national in scope:

The relation of employer and employee is a local relation. At common law, it is one of the domestic relations. The wages are paid for the doing of local work. Working conditions are obviously local conditions. The employees are not engaged in or about commerce, but exclusively in producing a commodity. And the controversies and evils, which it is the object of the act to regulate and minimize, are local controversies and evils affecting local work undertaken to accomplish that local result.

Two important elements of the paragraph above—the special local character and the importance of the common law—also featured prominently in Sutherland's zoning decision a decade previously.

Lost in the unfortunate tendency to lump together judges in blocs such as the "Four Horsemen" is the richness of Sutherland's contribution to Supreme Court jurisprudence and, unlike his two most notorious opinions, his enduring legacy as a skillful, clear-minded, and often independent jurist. His concern for individual liberty was not confined to the economic arena, as illustrated by his memorable and courageous opinion in *Powell v. Alabama* (1932), the decision that ordered new trials for the "Scottsboro Boys," nine African American teenagers who were falsely accused of raping two young white women in 1931. Breaking away from Justices Butler and McReynolds, as he did six years before in *Euclid v. Ambler*, Sutherland provided this picture of the nightmare that the defendants faced in state court:

The defendants, young, ignorant, illiterate, surrounded by hostile sentiment, haled back and forth under guard of soldiers, charged with an atrocious crime regarded with especial horror in the community where they were to be tried, were thus put in peril of their lives within a few moments after counsel for the first time charged with any degree of responsibility began to represent them.

Sutherland showed how the young men were denied the constitutionally protected "right to counsel in any substantial sense" by the third-rate performance of the defense attorneys:

It is not enough to assume that counsel thus precipitated into the case thought there was no defense, and exercised their best judgment in proceeding to trial without preparation. Neither they nor the court could say what a prompt and thoroughgoing investigation might disclose as to the facts. No attempt was made to investigate. No opportunity to do so was given. Defendants were immediately hurried to trial.

Sutherland supported his conclusion by a careful exploration of historical sources dating back to provisions in the earliest state constitutions and their precursors in English law. He overcame the hurdle of case law that suggested that the Bill of Rights protected criminal defendants from abuses by federal but not state officials. Because the right to counsel is "fundamental," he concluded, it had to be included in the notion of due process of law, if not in all criminal cases, at least "in a capital case, where the defendant is unable to employ counsel, and is incapable adequately of making his own defense because of ignorance, feeble mindedness, illiteracy, or the like." As in *Euclid v. Ambler*, Sutherland was not interested in painting with a broad brush. He was attentive to the details of the facts in the case before him, and those particular circumstances gave rise to the Court's important, though limited, holding.

In the decades following the publication of the Court's decision in *Euclid v. Ambler*, there has been considerable speculation as to why Sutherland broke from his more conservative colleagues. While this break was not unprecedented, as evidenced by *Powell v. Alabama*, it was unusual, particularly in a case with a widespread impact in which a property owner claimed that the government had violated its due process rights. Perhaps the justice's biography will shed light on the Euclidean puzzle.

To one of the chroniclers of Sutherland's life, Joel Francis Paschal, the justice was a passionate believer in individualism – "a man against the state." Sutherland was born in 1864 in Buckinghamshire, England, the son of a Scotsman who, after converting to the Church of Latter Day Saints, moved the family to Utah Territory. After the move, Sutherland's father abandoned his new religion, which meant that the son was raised as a nonbeliever in a Utah that then (as now) was dominated by Mormons. Sutherland followed three years at Brigham Young Academy (before it was a university) with work as a railroad agent. He attended law school at the University of Michigan in 1882, where he came under the influence of two important legal figures, both members of the state supreme court—Chief Justice James Campbell and Thomas M. Cooley, the author of the highly influential *Treatise on the Constitutional Limitations Which Rest upon the Legislative Power of the States of the American Union* (first published in 1868).

After practicing law in Provo, Sutherland moved to Salt Lake City and began a distinguished political career in 1896 when he was elected to the state's first legislature. Four years later, he was elected as a Republican to the U.S. House of Representatives; in 1905 he began serving the first of two terms in the U.S. Senate. Although in Congress Sutherland backed reform measures such as the Pure Food and Drug Act and workers compensation, he refused to break ranks with fellow Republicans in 1912 who endorsed Theodore Roosevelt's Progressive ticket, and he fought against many of President Woodrow Wilson's reform measures.

Having lost his Senate seat in 1916, he was elected as president of the American Bar Association (ABA) the following year. In his inaugural address, "Private Rights and Government Control," ABA President Sutherland stated that "doubts should be resolved in favor of the liberty of the individual" when the choice was "between the liberty of the citizen and the supposed good of the community." Given Sutherland's strong record of political and bar leadership, and a close friendship with Warren G. Harding, his former Senate colleague who was elected president in 1920, it was no real surprise when President Harding nominated the Utahan to the Supreme Court on September 5, 1922.

On the issue of Sutherland's refusal to strike down zoning as facially unconstitutional in *Euclid v. Ambler*, Paschal attributed the split among the often solid conservative bloc to the influence of the ideas of Herbert Spencer and Justice Cooley. According to this account, beginning in college and through his legal studies, Sutherland fell under the spell of Spencer's Social Darwinism:

> Spencer had said that the growth of numbers was responsible for the existence of the state at all. Hence, in a political context, overpopulation is no ordinary fact but one of an ultimate character, capable of justifying political power. The [zoning] statute, accord-

ingly, could not be considered unreasonable if the alleged congestion actually existed.

Paschal may well have exaggerated the influence of Spencer on Sutherland's thought, but he was on firmer ground when he noted the impact of Cooley, whose work allowed Sutherland to see "in the zoning act not the deprivation of property, but its enhancement." To Paschal, the justice's consistent adherence to his overriding judicial theory allowed him to see the benefits of zoning. "Had he been a creature of impulse, he might well have joined Butler, McReynolds, and Van Devanter" in striking down the village's ordinance.

The subtitle of a subsequent biographical study, Hadley Arkes's *The Return of George Sutherland: Restoring a Jurisprudence of Natural Rights*, suggested an alternative legal theory with which the justice was intimately associated. The ideas of Adam Smith and the Founders, who spoke of "unalienable rights," not Spencer and Cooley, provided the inspiration for Sutherland's jurisprudence, according to this alternative version. While Arkes wrote that generally Sutherland "supplied the most urban, moral defense of a free economy," to conservatives the "aberrant" opinion in *Euclid v. Ambler* is quite puzzling. "But," Arkes observed, "the puzzle dissolves once we recognize, again, that moral inclination, even among the conservative judges, to presume in favor of local regulations that are rooted in the genuine concerns of the police powers. For Sutherland, 'zoning' came to the Court with a momentum of respect, because it seemed to bear an obvious connection to the public health." Important also was the fact that zoning laws "would find their ground in the common law of 'nuisances.'"

Other commentators have, somewhat more unkindly, attributed Sutherland's support for zoning to his realization that this form of land-use regulation would be an effective device for maintaining the existing social order and keeping out racial and ethnic minorities. Despite a great deal of speculation of this sort, the solution to this enduring puzzle is most likely found in the political and legal status of zoning in 1926, the structure and words of the opinion itself, and the makeup of the majority in the case.

First, the forces that coalesced in support of zoning during the probusiness 1920s were by no means only Progressive or liberal in nature. Experts from many fields and politicians from all parties agreed that zoning was a positive system for achieving a well-planned community while maintaining and even enhancing property values. That widespread social and political support for zoning carried over in state legislature and courts in every region of the nation. State courts were in actuality following the Supreme Court's lead over the preceding two decades in leaving undisturbed land-use regulation passed by local elected officials. Height, area, and use regulation had quickly emerged as the status quo in America's cities and suburbs even as the case moved through the federal court system. The Herbert most readily identified in the American mind with the pro-zoning movement was Hoover, the Republican Secretary of Commerce, not Spencer.

Second, the organization of and discussion within the majority opinion made clear that this was a frontal attack on zoning upon enactment, not a case involving a landowner who had been fined or jailed for violating local law, who had been turned down for a building permit or a variance from the terms of the ordinance, or who had lost a sale because zoning went into effect. This fact alone distinguished *Euclid v. Ambler* from many cases in which a Court majority struck down a reform law as a violation of the due process clause. In the *Euclid v. Ambler* opinion, Sutherland emphasized that the outcome might be different in a concrete zoning enforcement situation, and only two years later he would write a unanimous opinion in favor of a landowner who actually suffered a loss because of the application of a zoning ordinance. That case was *Nectow v. City of Cambridge* (1928).

Third, Sutherland's was not the only conservative voice, or for that matter the only Harding selection, in the prozoning chorus. Looking back with the benefit of hindsight, the "yes" votes of Brandeis, Holmes, and Stone were not surprising, given their general sympathy (or tolerance) for reform and the reputation that this trio would soon earn as dissenters from some of the Court's more vehement antiregulatory decisions. The same could not be said of Chief Justice Taft and Justice Edward T. Sanford, however. Like Sutherland, these two other Harding nominees would at times vote to strike down reform measures, such as labor protections, as unconstitutional. In focusing attention on the one justice who wrote the majority opinion, commentators have lost sight of the fact that Taft and Sanford also broke ranks with their colleagues on the right. The vote of these three justices in *Euclid v. Ambler*, like Taft's and Sanford's dissent from Sutherland's decision in *Adkins* striking down a minimum wage law, illustrate the fluidity of judicial positions on the important issues of the day and the foolishness of pigeonholing justices into blocs and ideological categories seemingly set in stone. For many reasons, some simple and other complex, six individuals voted not to strike down Euclid's zoning ordinance, not one faction in support of a single legal theory. In this way, the collection of judges who approved zoning mirrored the diverse alliance that supported this popular form of regulating property use.

CHAPTER 7

The Immediate Aftermath

On Tuesday, November 23, 1926, the day after the Supreme Court announced the decision in *Euclid v. Ambler*, the *Cleveland Plain Dealer* featured two front-page articles on the local court dispute that had taken on national importance. One article was standard, postopinion fare: a short description of the holding, noting that the "right of municipalities to make and enforce regulations and laws for the zoning of property was sustained today by the supreme court of the United States," was followed by generous quotations from and a summary of the Court's opinion.

The other *Plain Dealer* article was pure parochial pride. The newspaper reported that 30 million Americans who lived in 440 cities that featured zoning, scattered among forty-one states, would feel the direct impact of the Court's holding in support of this newly blessed form of land-use regulation. The case was "entirely a Cleveland affair," given the local connections of Ambler Realty, Euclid, Metzenbaum, and Baker. Readers were provided with physical descriptions of the two litigators, both of whom were small in stature but not in ability. Metzenbaum was "a bantamweight, hardly more than five feet tall, and the supreme court justices had to crane their necks to see him over the edge of the bench." Likewise, Baker was "thin, spare and short, and for years has made fun of his size, especially when he was secretary of war and mayor."

Cleveland's city manager deemed the decision "almost revolutionary," which inspired the author of the article to take a glimpse one hundred years into the future, when, "instead of vast, spreading areas of factories, homes, parks, railroads, strewn together chaotically, without plan, with skylines varying according to the taste of the owners of the land, there may evolve cities where factories are segregated, where stores may be confined to certain heights, will have

{ 121 }

symmetry and architectural beauty, and admit the maximum air and light." One writer at least had found profound inspiration in Sutherland's ostensibly dry legal discourse.

Less effusive reports appeared in other Tuesday newspapers. The *Washington Post*, for example, carried an Associated Press article noting that the Cleveland suburb "won in the supreme court yesterday its right to enforce its zoning ordinance regulating the erection of buildings" and suggesting that the question of zoning's legitimacy was not yet fully resolved, as the Court's "decision was restricted to the specific question represented by the Euclid ordinance, and did not pass upon the validity of zoning regulations in general, which must be determined, the court stated, by the circumstances in each case." The *New York Times* that same day predicted that the Court's holding "will have an important bearing in New York and other large cities where questions relating to zoning have arisen." The *Wall Street Journal* buried its quick reference to the decision — "The zoning ordinance of Euclid, a suburb of Cleveland, Ohio, limiting the height, kind and use of building, etc., that may be erected in the village, was upheld by the Supreme Court as constitutional" — in an article summarizing several Supreme Court developments from November 22, chiefly the decisions on utility rate limitations and railroad regulation.

Later the same week, some of the nation's newspapers took the time to reflect on the wider implications of the decision. An editorial in the *New York Times* quoted Edward M. Bassett's effusive statement that *Euclid v. Ambler* was a "final and overwhelming victory." Turning its attention to local matters, the editorial speculated that, if the decision had gone the other way, "its effect might have been disastrous in" the state of New York. The newspaper then offered its hope that "some way may be found to give Jersey's municipalities the benefits of this up-to-date form of community action which has now been sanctioned by our highest court." As it turned out, not only would legislators and the judges in the Garden State jump on the zoning bandwagon, but within a couple of decades New Jersey would be America's leading jurisdiction on zoning law.

A *Washington Post* editorial stated that the decision was "of far-reaching importance" and observed that "municipal authorities and the general public may hail this ruling with the greatest satisfaction," while cautioning that "the courts should function" in the event zoning laws "containing unjust and discriminatory features" are passed. The editorial also included an important point about the potential benefits zoning presented for landowners, many of whom had opposed zoning restrictions: "Real estate operators should realize that in the larger sense zoning laws, establishing and maintaining property values, are to their advantage." The last point was reiterated in the same newspaper's "Washington Realtor" section two weeks later, as an article cited the National Association of Real Estate Boards (the organization that changed its name to the National Board of Realtors in 1974) for the proposition that the High Court's decision was "of the highest importance as affecting the conservation of real estate values in every municipality or government division where such provisions have been adopted." In this way the supporters of zoning were quick to point out that land-use regulation did not necessarily have the deleterious economic effect warned about by their opponents.

The Court's apparent shift away from a traditionally strict adherence to private property rights was not lost on the popular press. For example, a *Plain Dealer* editorial that appeared two days after the decision argued that "the decision is important as marking a more liberal attitude on the part of the federal court in its dealings with questions of property rights." *Euclid v. Ambler* was an indication that "the bourbon [that is, reactionary] view that the preservation of physical values is all-important no longer finds lodgment in our highest tribunal." In reality, several justices, including Sutherland, continued to hold an elevated, though certainly not absolute, view of private property rights.

As 1926 drew to a close, the *Christian Science Monitor* opined that the decision "seems to have attracted less public attention than its importance deserves." The writer contrasted ancient views of absolute ownership with the modern regulation of property and with British owners who "are considered as 'lords' of their possessions, however obtained." *Euclid v. Ambler* was instead the answer to an urban reformer's prayer, in that it would "strengthen the hands of those who are working to abolish the chaotic conditions existing in practically all the large cities of America" and "hasten the elimination of the 'slum' residential districts, which have been permitted to exist because of a supposition that the owners of the land had the right to use their property as they pleased." These very high hopes would be dashed, however, as urban America continued to wrestle with the serious challenges posed by economically distressed neighborhoods throughout the remainder of the twentieth century and beyond.

There was also no dramatic response in legal publications that appeared in the wake of *Euclid v. Ambler*. Most discussions of the case were simply descriptions of the holdings by lawyers in bar publications or by law students in student-edited law reviews. The most likely reason why legal commentary did not focus on the issues raised in the decision was that the debates over the constitutionality of zoning had appeared in the pages of the law reviews before the decision was handed down. After all, there was a gap of two years and ten months between the release of the district court and Supreme Court opinions. By late November 1926, many state courts had already rendered opinions on the zoning phenomenon.

The one exceptional law review commentary on *Euclid v. Ambler* appeared in the first volume of the *Cincinnati Law Review*, with the bland title, "The Decision of the Supreme Court of the United States in the Euclid Village Zoning Case." The author was "Alfred Bettman, of the Cincinnati Bar." This was not a piece in which the victorious side gloated. In fact, he seemed to be very sympathetic to one of the arguments on the landowner's behalf, although not the way in which the point was presented by Baker and Morgan. "The attorneys of the realty company," he wrote, "had a valid idea in their emphasis upon this metropolitan factor," the idea that "the fact of the location of a municipality within a metropolitan area has a bearing upon these factors of development trends, land values and appropriateness of use." However, counsel for the landowner "pushed this factor beyond its just deserts, and in the opinion of the Supreme Court that the suburban community is not required to merge its welfare completely in that of the metropolitan region is salutary and refreshing." Evidently Bettman's admiration for the opposition's arguments only went so far.

Bettman did offer that "there is ample ground for the suspicion that the Ambler Realty Company, while genuinely the party plaintiff, still represented a larger group seeking to destroy the zoning movement, and that the Euclid ordinance was chosen for this purpose because of certain weaknesses which were felt to inhere in its provisions." Luckily, the Supreme Court overlooked these "weaknesses," and "the decision and opinion of our highest court constitute for zoning and city planning a most important and joyful event." Bettman returned to the shortcomings of Euclid's ordinance, something that had troubled Bettman from the beginning, when he expressed "hope and trust" that the fact that the three dissenters wrote no opinion indicated that they "believe in the validity of zoning but were not convinced of the merits of the Euclid ordinance itself." One can imagine that Metzenbaum, who took pride in the ordinance that he helped draft, and in his defense of his village home, would have again objected to the arguments of his *amicus*.

In the meantime, the Supreme Court would soon decide other cases that would often draw the ire or admiration of the press and legal commentators, depending on which alliance of justices prevailed. The Taft Court in 1926 featured a contentious ideological lineup. By 1922, the Supreme Court included a core of four generally conservative justices: Willis Van Devanter, James McReynolds, George Sutherland, and Pierce Butler. These four, who often stood as bulwarks against government violations of property and contract rights, soon earned enduring (and occasionally unfair) reputations for being decidedly unfriendly to business regulation.

On the other end of the political spectrum sat Louis D. Brandeis, a Progressive lawyer from Boston with a national reputation. Though by no means an enemy of the private sector, Brandeis consistently favored statutory reforms of big business in the name of the greater good. As Edward Purcell has noted, Brandeis "focus[ed] his attention on the growing conflicts between large corporate interests on the one side and various groups of economic outsiders, including small business, on the other. He regarded concentrated power as overbearing and began to criticize 'bigness' in all its forms."

Justice Oliver Wendell Holmes, Jr., also generally indulged the whims of legislative majorities that passed reform measures, very few of which he personally supported. For his judicial, if not his personal, opinions, the independent-minded Boston Brahmin remained the hero of many Progressive activists, politicians, and theorists. In reality, as noted by Professor G. Edward White, Holmes's "personal sympathies were entirely with the capitalists. He not only considered them virtuous engines of social wealth; he had a kind of schoolboy's respect for their energy and will-power."

William Howard Taft was the victim of Progressive politics in the presidential campaign of 1912, in which as the Republican incumbent he was out-polled by his predecessor, Theodore Roosevelt (running on the Progressive ticket), and by the Democratic victor, Woodrow Wilson. In the campaign, Taft criticized Wilson for his "latitudinarian construction of the Constitution," which threatened "to weaken the protection it should afford against socialist raids upon property rights." Not surprisingly, as chief justice of the United States, Taft hoped that the conservative wing, along with moderate Justices Joseph McKenna, Edward Sanford, and Harlan Fiske Stone (who joined the Court upon McKenna's retirement in 1925), would enable Taft to shape a unified Court that would not be plagued by pesky dissents. That hope was frustrated, however, by Stone, the former Wall Street lawyer, who teamed with Holmes and Brandeis to form, according to Alpheus Thomas Mason, "the Three Musketeers [who] fought an unceasing battle against formalistic jurisprudence."

Euclid v. Ambler, with its deferential attitude toward government land-use regulators, appeared during a crucial transition period in American legal and constitutional history, as statutory and administrative law began to supplant the common law as the primary source of law governing business and private property relationships. The Progressive impulse to reform society and business was on a collision course with the due process clause of the Fourteenth Amendment, which mandated that no person could be deprived of "life, liberty, or property, without due process of law." Activist, conservative judges and their antiregulatory supporters broadly interpreted the term "liberty" in an effort to check government overreaching, holding most notably that the word included the right or freedom of contract. As a result, a large number of state and local statutory and regulatory schemes formed a sizable part of the Supreme Court's caseload for the first time in the tribunal's history. From the late 1890s through the mid-1930s, the justices heard hundreds of due process and related challenges.

A new form of "Progressive jurisprudence" evolved in the hands of judges, including the members of the Taft Court, who brought to the bench a worldview anchored in the strong belief in the dominance of the common law. These jurists were eager to draw lessons and insights from the centuries-old common law in their search for a mode of evaluating the constitutional legitimacy of the flood of new laws that were crafted and applied by elected officials and appointed administrative officials.

The members of the Taft Court brought special qualifications to the task of overseeing this crucial transition in the law. The backgrounds of these justices revealed strong links to the common law, as well as a special agility with new, superseding sources of legal authority that originated in the legislative chamber. Like their predecessors, these justices were attorneys who were educated and who engaged in practice during a period when the common law was predominant. Several justices, including McKenna, Holmes, William Day, Van Devanter, Mahlon Pitney, John Clarke, Taft, and Sanford, had helped to shape and adapt the common law from the bench before their elevation to the U.S. Supreme Court.

Moreover, during this crucial transition period, several justices before they reached the High Court had played key roles in the development of the new administrative state. They brought to their work on the Court valuable experiences as elected and appointed officials, with first-hand knowledge of the growth of the regulatory state generally and of reform legislation and its implementation specifically. For example, Justice Sutherland had served in both chambers of Congress between 1901 and 1917, following four years of service in the newly formed Utah State Senate. Although he was not identified with the Progressive wing of the Republican Party, Sutherland at times supported reform statutes in the state and federal legislatures, including the maximum hours legislation for underground miners in Utah that the Supreme Court in 1898 upheld in *Holden v. Hardy*. In that decision, Justice Henry B. Brown was dismissive of a due process challenge:

> This right of contract . . . is itself subject to certain limitations which the State may lawfully impose in the exercise of its police powers. While this power is inherent in all governments, it has doubtless been greatly expanded in its application during the past century, owing to an enormous increase in the number of occupations which are dangerous, or so far detrimental to the health of

employes as to demand special precautions for their well-being and protection, or the safety of adjacent property.

Sutherland and his legislative colleagues would certainly have appreciated the High Court's deferential attitude.

Justice Brandeis's achievements before his controversial appointment to the High Court included skillful and innovative advocacy on behalf of reform efforts. He will always be identified with the "Brandeis Brief," the compilation of extralegal information that helped carry the day in 1908's *Muller v. Oregon*, which upheld maximum hours legislation for women.

Several justices held cabinet positions in their pre-Court careers. Former U.S. attorneys general McReynolds and Stone had each directed the growing bureaucracy in the Department of Justice before they joined the Court. During the Spanish-American War, Justice Day had served for a few months as secretary of state, while Taft was secretary of war before his move to the White House.

By the middle of the nineteenth century, American judges had already demonstrated their confidence in the elasticity and adaptability of many centuries-old, judge-made legal concepts. These judges believed deeply in the crucial role that judicial interpretation from the past played in solving the problems of the present and in the ability of the common law to respond to profound technological, economic, and demographic changes. Probably the most sound and memorable example of that philosophy can be found in *Norway Plains Co. v. Boston & Maine Railroad*, an 1854 Massachusetts Supreme Judicial Court opinion written by Chief Justice Lemuel Shaw (known to many readers of American literature as the father-in-law of Herman Melville). Shaw observed that "when a new practice or new course of business arises, the rights and duties of parties are not without a law to govern them; the general considerations of reason, justice and policy, which underlie the particular rules of the common law, will still apply, modified and adapted, by the same considerations, to the new circumstances." Before the dawn of the "age of statutes," common law judges such as Chief Justice Shaw were extremely confident that common law rules could be molded to govern modern conditions without violating "the general considerations of reason, justice and policy, which underlie" those very rules.

More than fifty years later, in defense of a federal postal savings-bank bill, a Republican U.S. Senator from Utah articulated Shaw-like optimism concerning the adaptability of federal constitutional law to rapidly changing society and legal conditions. During congressional debate in 1910, the lawmaker asserted, "While it is true that the Constitution continues to speak with its original words and meaning, their scope and application continually broaden so as to include new conditions, instrumentalities, and activities." That senator was George Sutherland, who, as a Supreme Court Justice, was not daunted by the spate of land-use regulation that preceded and foreshadowed the litigation in *Euclid v. Ambler*.

Sixteen years after his statement in the Senate, that judicial opinion would echo Sutherland's ideas and actual phrases:

> Regulations, the wisdom, necessity and validity of which, as applied to existing conditions, are so apparent that they are now uniformly sustained, a century ago, or even half a century ago, probably would have been rejected as arbitrary and oppressive. . . . While the meaning of constitutional guaranties never varies, the scope of their application must expand or contract to meet the new and different conditions which are constantly coming within the field of their operation. In a changing world, it is impossible that it should be otherwise. But although a degree of elasticity is thus imparted, not to the *meaning*, but to the *application* of constitutional principles, statutes and ordinances, which, after giving due weight to the new conditions, are found clearly not to conform to the Constitution, of course, must fall.

With their feet firmly planted in this common law soil, and with important practical experience in the emerging legal landscape dominated by statutes and regulations, the members of the Taft Court did a masterful job of mining useful Anglo-American legal nuggets such as nuisance law in *Euclid v. Ambler*.

Justice Sutherland, like other members of the Taft Court, recognized that the world around them was changing at a rapid pace and that judges could not predict with accuracy what factual and legal situations might lead to unfairness and injustice even in the near future. These judges were facing unprecedented developments — profound demographic shifts caused by millions of immigrants from southern and eastern Europe; new political configurations such as the momentous split in the Republican Party in 1912 and the growth of influential third parties; scientific inventions that accelerated dramatically the flow of people, culture, and information; and the repercussions of the nation's mobilization for and involvement in World War I.

Inside this whirlwind of profound change, the Court in *Euclid v. Ambler* accorded popularly elected officials a strong presumption of correctness. Perhaps the justices were beginning to realize that the judiciary's place was at the boundaries of public policy debates, not at the center, and that the judge's role was to check the occasional, serious abuses of the other, coequal branches.

This is not to suggest that an abrupt shift occurred on November 22, 1926. Rather, the split decision in *Euclid v. Ambler* indicates that the Taft Court was wrestling with the difficult task of deciding when deference was warranted and when the Constitution commanded judicial protection of cherished property rights. Only four years before its decision dismissing Ambler Realty's claims, the Taft Court found that the state of Pennsylvania had exceeded the reach of its police power when it passed the Kohler Act, a statute that prevented a coal company from mining if it caused subsidence of structures on the surface. Justice Holmes, in his opinion for the eight-member majority in *Pennsylvania Coal Co. v. Mahon*, wrote this memorable sentence, which provides inspiration to private property rights advocates to this day: "The general rule at least is, that while property may be regulated to a certain extent, if regulation goes too far it will be recognized as a taking." Because the Takings Clause of the Fifth Amendment outlaws such takings unless just compensation is paid to the property owner (in this instance, the coal company did not receive any compensation), the statute was unconstitutional.

The holding in *Pennsylvania Coal* appears to have less in common with the result in *Euclid v. Ambler* than it did with antireform decisions such as *Adkins v. Children's Hospital*, the 1923 case invalidating the District of Columbia's minimum wage for women and children. In that case, Justice Sutherland wrote, for a five-member majority: "There is, of course, no such thing as absolute freedom of contract. It is subject to a great variety of restraints. But freedom of contract is, nevertheless, the general rule and restraint the exception; and the exercise of legislative authority to abridge it can be justified only by the existence of exceptional circumstances." Those circumstances apparently were absent in the *Adkins* case, as they were in other controversial contract and property rights cases that came before the Court until old age (and not necessarily President Franklin Roosevelt's inadvisable court-packing attempt) took its toll on the bench during the New Deal.

One might have predicted with confidence that decisions such as *Pennsylvania Coal* and *Adkins* would have made precarious the Village of Euclid's attempt to defend its zoning ordinance over the constitutional objections of a landowner. That prediction came true, at least in part, when Judge Westenhaver announced his opinion in the lower court, which relied on both precedents:

> The courts never hesitate to look through the false pretense to the substance. As instances in which false pretenses of exercising police power in the interests of public health, safety, morals, and welfare, were disregarded, attention is called to *Pennsylvania Coal Co. v. Mahon* and *Adkins v. Children's Hospital.* In the last case, a wider acquiescence in the assumed police power was shown than can be asserted in behalf of the power here involved.

Nevertheless, despite references in the lower court's opinion and in briefs filed by Baker, Metzenbaum, and Bettman, neither precedent was cited in the Supreme Court's opinion in *Euclid v. Ambler.*

In reality, despite its pro–property rights holding, *Pennsylvania Coal* was not cited in any of the four zoning decisions that the Supreme Court rendered between 1926 and 1928. Justice Holmes's "general rule" apparently did not have a dramatic impact on how the Court analyzed the legitimacy of regulations affecting the use and development of land in the years immediately following the issuance of his opinion.

Baker, in a letter to a correspondent in Minneapolis dated December 6, 1926, offered this prediction: "I think the Supreme Court, having now stated the police power in its largest possible terms, will spend some years limiting the doctrine by adverse holdings in unreasonable instances." Once again, as with his early prediction regarding a positive outcome in *Euclid v. Ambler*, Baker's crystal ball let him down.

On March 21, 1927, in *Beery v. Houghton*, the Court affirmed a pro-zoning decision by the Supreme Court of Minnesota (allowing Minneapolis to exclude "a four-family flat building from a designated residential district") by simply citing *Euclid v. Ambler*. Within two years after the Court announced its decision in *Euclid v. Ambler*, the justices presented full, unanimous opinions, all written by Justice Sutherland, in three other cases involving constitutional challenges to zoning. In *Zahn v. Board of Public Works*, the justices affirmed a decision of the California Supreme Court. The Court thus denied relief to a landowner challenging a Los Angeles zoning ordinance that did not allow the plaintiffs to use their property for business purposes. Euclidean deference was the key to the Court's decision on May 16, 1927: "The most that can be said is that whether that determination [the zoning designation] was an unreasonable, arbitrary or unequal exercise of power is fairly debatable. In such circumstances, the settled rule of this court is that it will not substitute its judgment for that of the legislative body charged with the primary duty and responsibility of determining the question."

Two weeks later, in *Gorieb v. Fox*, the Court upheld a local setback regulation from Roanoke, Virginia. This opinion also echoed the rationale of *Euclid v. Ambler*:

> It is hard to see any controlling difference between regulations which require the lot-owner to leave open areas at the sides and rear of his house and limit the extent of his use of the space above his lot and a regulation which requires him to set his building a reasonable distance back from the street. Each interferes in the same way, if not to the same extent, with the owner's general right of dominion over his property. All rest for their justification upon the same reasons which have arisen in recent times as a result of the great increase and concentration of population in urban communities and the vast changes in the extent and complexity of the problems of modern city life.

The final case in the zoning quartet, *Nectow v. City of Cambridge*, proved a winner for the landowner of a vacant lot upon which a mansion once sat. The owner had received an offer of $63,000 for the parcel, but the purchaser backed out when a zoning ordinance was passed that, for a section of the property, disallowed the kind business and industrial uses already present in the neighborhood. The landowner's attempts to secure a zoning amendment and a variance were unsuccessful, so he brought suit in state court seeking relief from the zoning ordinance. The trial court referred the matter to a special master who found that "that no practical use can be made of the land in question for residential purposes, because among other reasons herein related, there would not be adequate return on the amount of any investment for the development of the property," and that "the districting of the plaintiff's land in a residence district would not promote the health, safety, convenience and general welfare of the inhabitants of that part of" Cambridge, Massachusetts. Nevertheless, the trial court sided with the city, and the Supreme Judicial Court of Massachusetts affirmed, noting, "we do not feel justified in holding that the zoning line established is whimsical and without foundation in reason. In our opinion it is not violative of the rights secured to the plaintiff either by the Constitution of this Commonwealth or by the Fourteenth Amendment to the Constitution of the United States." On May 14, 1928, the U.S. Supreme Court reversed, citing with approval the master's finding and deeming "the invasion of the property of plaintiff . . . serious and highly injurious."

With the exception of *Goldblatt v. Town of Hempstead*, a 1962 case in which the Court upheld a Long Island town's regulation of dredging and pit excavation, the Supreme Court was out of the zoning review business for the four decades following this warning shot fired in *Nectow*. It would be the primary responsibility of state and lower federal courts, which also as a rule followed the lead of *Euclid v. Ambler*, to determine the legitimacy of zoning as it affected the community and specific landowners.

Within a few years after the *Euclid v. Ambler* holding was announced, the states that had indicated an antipathy toward zoning fell into line, either by judicial opinions as in New Jersey, Maryland, and Texas, or by a constitutional amendment specifically authorizing this form of regulation, as was the case in Georgia. While Ambler Realty's federal court challenge was making its way slowly to a final decision, Baker and Morgan wrote an *amicus* brief in opposition to zoning in *Pritz v. Messer*. In May, 1925, the Supreme Court of Ohio held that in theory the Columbus zoning ordinance was not unconstitutional, although the court prevented one landowner from using the ordinance to stop another owner from changing his property to a four-apartment residence. Filing a friend of the court brief on the other side of the dispute was Bettman, who would have been pleased with the discussion of zoning's basic constitutionality, even if that discussion was not needed to resolve the dispute between the parties.

There were cases in which municipalities were sanctioned for wielding their power in an unreasonable, arbitrary, or confiscatory fashion, but they were certainly the exceptions much more than the rule. One such case was the challenge Baker brought against the Village of University Heights on behalf of the Jewish orphanage. In 1927, the federal appeals court affirmed a lower court decision, written by Baker's good friend Westenhaver, that favored the Cleveland Jewish Orphans' home, but not on the grounds of religious discrimination. Adhering to the framework that the Supreme Court set out in its decision the year before in *Euclid v. Ambler*, the appeals court concluded, "We do not doubt that the ordinance is a valid enactment in its general aspects, but as applied to this case it is, we think, unreasonable." Under the new jurisdictional rules, the village attempted to bring its case to the Supreme Court, but the justices denied certiorari, putting an end to the dispute. For the most part, however, federal and state judges, even in states that seemingly cherished a strong attachment to private property rights, were sending a strong message that, in line with Euclidean deference, they did not wish to sit as a judicial version of the zoning board of appeals.

CHAPTER 8

Confronting the Consequences of Zoning in Action

The written judicial opinion is the lifeblood of the Anglo-American system of common (that is, judge-made) law. Sometimes a very special opinion becomes an important symbol in the eyes of judges, teachers, practitioners, and scholars. Within the pages and paragraphs of these iconic cases, the careful reader can perceive the dominant themes, the persistent pattern of decision making, the extralegal underpinnings, and the operative vocabulary of a discrete area of the law. *Euclid v. Ambler* is the central opinion of land-use law and has been ever since it was announced in the fall of 1926.

The case is best known by one party's name — "Euclid" — which is a name that suggests to the layperson the lines, points, and planes of elementary geometry. The importance of Justice Sutherland's opinion, taking up nineteen pages in the *United States Reports*, is indisputable: many articles in law, planning, economics, and historical journals have been written to explain the case, and scholars continue to debate its import and value more than eighty years after the event. Thousands of federal and state cases at trial and appellate levels have cited the opinion, and even in the twenty-first century it is prominently displayed in law school casebooks and texts from related disciplines such as planning and urban studies. Legal treatises and hornbooks in areas such as land use, local government, constitutional, and property law discuss the decision, often in great detail, and, even after several decades of evolutionary developments in planning and zoning practice, lawyers still use the term "Euclidean" to describe the system of height, area, and use regulation that the Supreme Court approved in 1926.

The centrality of *Euclid v. Ambler* goes beyond the traditional measures noted in the paragraph above. Justice Sutherland's opinion, unlike such famous and notorious cases as *Dred Scott v. Sandford*, which shamefully denied the American citizenship of African Americans in 1857, is much more than a milestone or a reference point that is cited out of habit or to appeal to the reader's or audience's familiarity after generations of use. The challenge brought by the Ambler Realty Company remains very relevant to students and professionals alike in many fields. The student who truly masters the text of the opinion has a firm grip on the fundamental rules and rationales found in thousands of succeeding cases. To this day, the typical land-use dispute pits a disgruntled property owner against local government officials who at least allegedly have failed to appreciate the extent of the economic harm caused by their acts or failures to act. In some instances, the complaint is filed by the equally disgruntled neighbors of other property owners who benefited from a generous decision by public officials. Regardless of who won in the first round, however, the principles of *Euclid v. Ambler* are bound to play a role in any judicial review of the decision made by local and state land-use regulators.

There are three key, intrinsic elements of the 1926 opinion that best explain its ability to withstand the challenges wrought by the passage of time; by significant political and theoretical shifts; and by the profound changes Americans have experienced since the Jazz Age of flappers, the Charleston, and speakeasies. First, the majority of Taft Court justices sent a signal that the judicial branch endorsed a flexible approach to the legislative implementation and judicial review of public land-use planning tools. Rather than serving as a zoning oversight commission, looking over the shoulders of local officials when they draft and enforce zoning ordinances, the justices deferred to local elected and appointed officials, reserving the right to step in only in particularly egregious or confiscatory instances.

Second, the Court in *Euclid v. Ambler* endorsed a careful, expert-based approach to the regulation of land use, allowing the nation's states and municipalities to experiment with administrative alternatives to the vagaries of the market and to age-old common-law rules for resolving disputes between neighbors. No longer would legal officials have to wait until harm occurred, either to a neighbor or to the community at large. Nor would real estate developers have to rely on legal principles developed long before the invention of the automobile and before the rise of the modern, administrative state to create and maintain well-planned residential neighborhoods.

Third, the majority in *Euclid v. Ambler* approved the transfer of development rights over and above a level often labeled "reasonable rate of return" from individual to collective ownership. In other words, as long as government officials did not use zoning controls to prevent landowners from realizing a fair return on their initial investment, the judiciary would not interfere. The Supreme Court made clear that, laissez-faire myths to the contrary, Americans do not have a constitutionally protected right to receive the maximum profit from their real estate investments.

This last point is perhaps the most important one as our expanding population faces familiar and newly identified environmental harms above and below the ground and water, in the air that we breathe, and in the atmosphere that affects our climate. Even at a time when American judges, politicians, and media pundits celebrate the fundamental nature of private property rights, *Euclid v. Ambler* reminds us that states have granted the most modest local governments the authority to enact and enforce measures that affect the value of land, sometimes quite dramatically. In the last few decades, the "Euclidean" principle of judicial deference to government regulators has provided a protective shield for a wide variety of environmental controls, so long as officials developing and enforcing those controls are acting, as *Euclid v. Ambler* instructs, in support of the public health, safety, morals, and general welfare, in ways that are not arbitrary, capricious, or unreasonable.

The decision in *Euclid v. Ambler* is important as well for the way in which the words and phrases of Justice Sutherland's opinion actually anticipate the four principal, "modern" objections that opponents have raised to Euclidean zoning and to comprehensive land-use regulation. Indeed, to study the opinion absent some appreciation of the four "seeds" that were planted in *Euclid v. Ambler* — exclusion, anticompetitiveness, parochialism, and aestheticism — is to blind oneself to the negative side of zoning that has always threatened its overall benefit to society.

Excluding Undesirable People and Uses

Exclusion was the essence of Euclidean zoning. In Justice Sutherland's words, "the crux of the more recent zoning legislation [was] the creation and maintenance of residential districts, from which business and trade of every sort, including hotels and apartments, are excluded." Structures and parcels were classified according to the height, area, and uses that are deemed appropriate for each specific location. For example, according to the Village of Euclid's 1922 "comprehensive zoning plan," the U-1 classification excluded the highest number of potential uses. Only the following were allowed: "single family dwellings, public parks, water towers and reservoirs, suburban and interurban electric railway passenger stations and rights of way, and farming, non-commercial greenhouse nurseries and truck gardening."

The insulation of single-family residences was an attempt to use the power of the state to regulate land uses more rigidly and effectively than had been the case with private devices, particularly covenants and private nuisance actions. No longer, zoning advocates hoped, would the character of the neighborhood depend on the whims of developers or the insistence or vigilance of neighbors. Local government officials — planners, commissioners, inspectors — would devise and enforce a properly legislated zoning plan.

From its origins, American zoning has been used to exclude and separate supposedly "offensive" uses and people, particularly racial and ethnic minorities. The link between land-use regulation and anti-ethnic feelings had been acknowledged by the Supreme Court forty years before the decision in *Euclid v. Ambler*. In *Yick Wo v. Hopkins* (1886), the Court ordered the release from custody of two Chinese aliens who had been imprisoned for violating an 1880 San Francisco ordinance that read, in part,

> It shall be unlawful, from and after the passage of this order, for any person or persons to establish, maintain, or carry on a laundry within the corporate limits of the city and county of San Francisco without having first obtained the consent of the board of supervisors, except the same be located in a building constructed either of brick or stone.

While such regulatory restraint on the use of one's property might appear to be quite a legitimate exercise of the police power, particularly in a city that, with hindsight, we know was a conflagration waiting to happen, the officials' race-based, selective enforcement of the ordinance amounted to a constitutional violation. Justice Stanley Matthews pointed out that, while the city had denied permission to two hundred Chinese nationals, eighty non-Chinese launderers had been "permitted to carry on the same business under similar conditions." The unanimous court concluded: "The fact of this discrimination is admitted. No reason for it is shown, and the conclusion cannot be resisted, that no reason for it exists except hostility to the race and nationality to which the petitioners belong, and which in the eye of the law is not justified."

That the crucial issue before the Court in *Yick Wo* was the method of enforcement and not the discriminatory effect was made clear in the opinion and in a comparison with the Court's holding in a case from the previous year, *Soon Hing v. Crowley*. Prosecuted under a different San Francisco ordinance prohibiting the operation of public laundries and washhouses between the hours of 10 p.m. and 6 a.m., Soon Hing's plea fell on deaf ears:

> The petition alleges that it [the ordinance] was adopted owing to a feeling of antipathy and hatred prevailing in the city and county of San Francisco against the subjects of the Emperor of China resident therein, and for the purpose of compelling those engaged in the laundry business to abandon their lawful vocation, and residence there, and not for any sanitary, police, or other legitimate purpose. There is nothing, however, in the language of the ordinance, or in the record of its enactment, which in any respect tends to sustain this allegation. . . . The motives of the legislators, considered as the purposes they had in view, will always be presumed to be to accomplish that which follows as the natural and reasonable effect of their enactments.

This constitutional challenge came up short. Yet, the link between police power regulation of the use of private property and ethnic discrimination was fixed in the memory of the High Court.

While the justices might not be convinced fully as to the invalidity of regulations that only indirectly discriminated against racial and ethnic minorities, the Court held otherwise when faced with explicit racial zoning by means of a city ordinance. In *Buchanan v. Warley*, a 1917 decision invalidating Louisville's ordinance forbidding African Americans to move into a predominantly white neighborhood and whites to move into a predominantly African American neighborhood, the Supreme Court set aside the regulation ostensibly designed "to promote the public peace by preventing racial conflicts." A unanimous Court, in an opinion by Justice William R. Day, expressed its belief that "this attempt to prevent the alienation of the property in question to a person of color was not a legitimate exercise of the police power of the State, and is in direct violation of the fundamental law enacted in the Fourteenth Amendment of the Constitution preventing state interference with property rights except by due process of law." Despite the undeniable link between the Equal Protection Clause and the history of racial discrimination against African Americans, the Court relied instead on the private property rights protected by the Due Process Clause found in the Fourteenth Amendment. Thus, by the time zoning challenges became popular in state and lower federal courts, American judges were quite aware of the actual or potential use of governmental property restrictions to discriminate against immigrants, ethnic minorities, and for that matter any other group out of favor with those holding the political reins.

The less than holy alliance between zoning as a particular land-use planning tool and anti-immigrant sentiment dates back to the birthplace of American height, area, and use zoning—New York City. As has been ably demonstrated by Seymour Toll in *Zoned American*, one of the driving forces behind passage of New York's 1916 ordinance was a coalition of Fifth Avenue retailers. The garment industry that had worked its way up the avenue over the preceding few decades, with its mass of eastern European workers, posed a serious threat to the future of high-class retailing: "It sought the same thing as the carriage trade merchant—gain—but its route was the tall loft building, its generals were real estate speculators, and its troops were lower East Side immigrants."

The metaphor employed by one key spokesman for the Fifth Avenue Association was far from flattering (and very revealing):

"Gentlemen, you are like cattle in a pasture, and the needle trade workers are the flies that follow you from one pasture to another, nagging you in to abandoning one great centre after another and leaving a trail of ruin, devastation, and bankruptcy up and down the length of the city." The metaphor was reminiscent of Henry James's impressions from a visit to New York City less than two decades before. In *The American Scene* (1907), James wrote of "the sense, after all, of a great swarming, a swarming that had begun to thicken, infinitely, as soon as we had crossed to the East side. . . . There is no swarming like that of Israel when once Israel has got a start, and the scene here bristled, at every step, with the signs and sounds, immitigable, unmistakable, of a Jewry that had burst all bounds."

Echoes of this entomological imagery reverberate in Justice Sutherland's opinion in *Euclid v. Ambler*. How far from the metaphor of swarming flies is Sutherland's characterization of an apartment house as "a mere parasite, constructed in order to take advantage of . . . open spaces and attractive surroundings"? It is probably close enough to warrant speculation that the tides (only recently receded owing to immigration restrictions in the early 1920s) of "new immigrants" from southern and eastern Europe, many of whom were current or potential residents of hotels and apartments in the Cleveland region as in other large cities, in part inspired the Court's support for the constitutionality of comprehensive land-use controls. Moreover, Justice Sutherland converted a "neutral" reference in Alfred Bettman's *amicus* brief to a furnace in a living room into the most memorable chestnut from *Euclid v. Ambler*: "A nuisance may be merely a right thing in the wrong place, — like a pig in the parlor instead of the barnyard."

That the members of the Taft Court were aware of the socioeconomic and discriminatory aspects of zoning is undeniable. As the justices reviewed Judge Westenhaver's opinion in *Ambler Realty Company v. Village of Euclid*, they should have pondered this direct allusion to the exclusionary purpose and potential of zoning:

The purpose to be accomplished [by the zoning ordinance] is really to regulate the mode of living of persons who may hereafter inhabit it [Euclid]. In the last analysis, the result to be accomplished is to classify the population and segregate them according to their income or situation in life. The true reason why some persons live in a mansion and others in a shack, why some live in a single-family dwelling and others in a double-family dwelling, why some live in a two-family dwelling and others in an apartment, or why some live in a well-kept apartment and others in a tenement, is primarily economic. It is a matter of income and wealth, plus the labor and difficulty of procuring adequate domestic service.

Indeed, Westenhaver's prediction of what would have happened had *Buchanan v. Warley* gone the other way provided the Supreme Court with an important, prescient insight into zoning's exclusionary potential. "It is equally apparent," Westenhaver wrote, "that the next step in the exercise of this police power would be to apply similar restrictions for the purpose of segregating in like manner various groups of newly arrived immigrants. The blighting of property values and the congestion of population, whenever the colored or certain foreign races invade a residential section, are so well known as to be within the judicial cognizance." One of the major results of the perception that this "invasion" threatened property values was the "white flight" phenomenon in many American cities that began in many American cities in the post–World War II decades and picked up steam after court-ordered school busing in the 1970s. Aided and abetted by banks and insurance companies that engaged in discriminatory practices (redlining), by real estate agents who orchestrated a sales panic among white homeowners when an African American family moved into their neighborhood (blockbusting), and by federal housing, tax, and highway construction programs that favored new suburban construction over revitalization of urban neighborhoods, many white, middle-class city-dwellers found themselves safely ensconced in bedroom communities that featured single-family residential zones protected by exclusionary devices such as minimum lot size requirements and bans on mobile, manufactured, and other low-cost housing.

Nearly five decades after Judge Westenhaver's prediction, the supreme court of New Jersey dropped a bombshell on the law and planning community. In its 1975 opinion in *Southern Burlington County N.A.A.C.P. v. Township of Mount Laurel*, this highly respected state tribunal recognized and attacked head-on the link between land-use restrictions and socioeconomic discrimination. This undeniable connection was particularly distasteful because of the state's "crisis – a desperate need for housing, especially of decent living accommodations economically suitable for low and moderate income communities." To a small group of commentators such as Charles Haar and Norman Williams, who had perceived this connection early in the 1950s, *Mount Laurel* was an appropriate, if somewhat delayed, judicial response. To a much larger number of critics and skeptics, particularly local and state legislators and hesitant judges on other courts, New Jersey's justices were mistaken arbiters at best, socialist usurpers at worst.

New Jersey's legal struggle against exclusionary zoning did not end in 1975. The state supreme court has revisited the topic several times since, and in the 1980s the state legislature passed a Fair Housing Act that augmented (and partially watered down) the judiciary's remedial efforts. While a few other states cautiously followed the Garden State's lead in the courts and legislative chambers – notably Pennsylvania, New York, California, and Massachusetts – for the most part in those and the remaining states, local governments are given great leeway in erecting zoning barriers to outsiders from the lower rungs of the socioeconomic ladder.

The careful student of the Court's opinion in *Euclid v. Ambler* cannot feign surprise at these more recent developments, for the potential use of governmental property restrictions, similarly to the private, racially restrictive covenants used by the Van Sweringens and their counterparts throughout the nation that the Supreme Court found unconstitutional in *Shelley v. Kraemer* (1948), was one of the seeds planted in Justice Sutherland's opinion. Buried between the constitutional catchwords and sociological shibboleths were the loaded words and phrases, and a tradition, of segregation and exclusion.

Tampering with the Market

The second seed planted in *Euclid v. Ambler* was the government's use of regulatory power to control or eliminate competition in the real estate market. The relatively unrestrained market in industrial and commercial sites in metropolitan Cleveland was one of the first victims of Euclid's comprehensive zoning ordinance, at least according to Ambler Realty and its allies. Not only was part of Ambler's piece of real estate, nestled between Euclid Avenue and the Nickel Plate Road, severely devalued (at least according to its owner), but also certain unnamed parties would have virtual monopolies on the most intensive (and therefore most potentially lucrative) uses permitted on those selected, choice lots in the suburb that were properly zoned, at least for the foreseeable future. According to Judge Westenhaver, "The plain truth is that the true object of the ordinance in question is to place all the property in an undeveloped area of 16 square miles in a strait-jacket."

This second seed has blossomed into two sets of challenges to Euclidean zoning. First, in the decades following the Court's approval of zoning in theory, many jurisdictions wrestled with the practical problem left unresolved in the earliest ordinances—the nonconforming use. The preexisting gas station, repair shop, or laundry that ended up being surrounded by block after block of homes in an area of town that was, for the first time, zoned for residential use only, could monopolize business within its artificially created, captive market. The government officials who in their wisdom isolated the nonconforming use with a fervent prayer that it would just disappear, actually freed the owner from the burdens of competition that it may well have experienced if the zone had been set aside for commercial pursuits.

When it became apparent in the 1950s that those prayers were not being answered, zoning supporters chose two basic different tactics for reducing the number of, or even eliminating, nagging nonconformities. Most municipalities adopted rules that have severely restricted modifications of the preexisting use. For example, local ordinances typically provide that discontinuing, abandoning, expanding, extending, enlarging, reconstructing, or altering the use will result in a loss of the right to continue the nonconformity. The second, and more controversial tactic, was to amortize the nonconforming use by identifying a date or time period after which the owner loses the right to continue the "offending" use. While both tactics have generally been accepted by the nation's courts, a few judges have expressed concern that amortization could amount to an unconstitutional taking.

The second body of zoning and land-use law that has sprouted from the anticompetitive seed was inspired largely by two controversial Supreme Court antitrust cases: *City of Lafayette v. Louisiana Power & Light* (1978), and *Community Communications Co. v. City of Boulder* (1982). The justices' rulings on alleged utilities and franchise abuses suggested that a municipality's zoning authorities and a favored property owner might possibly be involved in an illegal conspiracy to restrain trade. For example, would it not be a violation of the federal or state antitrust laws for a city that was involved in a public-private partnership to redevelop a central business district's shopping area to deny a zoning change to an owner-developer who proposed to build a competing regional shopping mall on the outskirts of the city?

When an Illinois federal district court entered a $38 million judgment against local governments that allegedly conspired to deprive a developer of a hookup to a public sewer system, chills went down the spines of local government officials throughout the nation. A number of state legislatures reacted to this perceived threat to the financial health of American localities by extending the state's exemption from antitrust liability to local governments, while Congress enacted the Local Government Antitrust Act in 1984 to remove the threat of treble damages in future cases.

It might seem ironic, given the rich trust-busting image of late nineteenth and early twentieth century reformers, that a program with Progressive roots would have such a strong anticompetitive potential. What is often forgotten in our haste to generalize about and stereotype political movements is that before World War I public monopolies were often considered the solution to many private sector abuses. So, for example, Frederic Howe and Newton D. Baker championed municipal ownership of lucrative utilities as a way to avoid the corruption that plagued the awarding of franchises by urban political machines.

It helps to understand zoning as a variation on this municipal ownership theme, for local governments, especially in the new suburbs not yet swallowed by annexation, in effect retained control of land development rights through comprehensive land-use planning and the restriction of uses. It became the obligation of the judiciary to assure that graft and corruption did not infest the zoning function as it had the awarding of franchises in an earlier period.

The anticompetitive component of zoning also suggests that the urban reformers who advanced the cause of land-use planning were not solely responsible for the popularity of height, area, and use zoning. It is important to recognize that vested real estate interests, such as the Fifth Avenue merchants in Manhattan or the industry representative who participated in the Advisory Committee on City Planning and Zoning, played (and continue to play) an important role in developing and maintaining comprehensive zoning. In other words, the attractiveness and enhanced value of an area that is set aside as the only available industrial or commercial property were probably hard to overcome in the minds of many influential, conservative property owners (and judges) who were otherwise predisposed to oppose government regulation of land ownership and use.

Resisting Regionalism

Euclid v. Ambler's third seed, parochialism, is best captured by Justice Sutherland's observation that "the village, though physically a suburb of Cleveland, is politically a separate municipality, with powers of its own and authority to govern itself as it sees fit within the limits of the organic law of its creation and the State and Federal Constitutions." In many ways, the Court's 1926 decision cleared the way for similarly situated communities to limit their population and to ward off the evils of urbanization, despite the fact that the municipality, like the Village of Euclid, stood in the way of the natural flow of affordable housing for central city residents hoping to escape the physical confinement and the social, economic, and political problems of inner-city life.

As noted in Chapter 3, the use of public and private land-use controls was closely connected to the growth of politically distinct suburbs throughout the nation. In the words of an anti-annexation editorial from a Chicago suburban newspaper quoted by Kenneth T. Jackson: "Under local government we can absolutely control every objectionable thing that may try to enter our limits—but once annexed we are at the mercy of city hall." Sam Bass Warner, Jr.'s insights regarding greater Boston's history in the late nineteenth century remain instructive:

> Beyond Boston the special suburban form of popularly managed local government continued to flourish. In suburbs of substantial income and limited class structure, high standards of education and public service were often achieved. Each town, however, now managed its affairs as best it could surrounded by forces largely beyond its control.

By the 1920s, zoning would provide a significant means of control; at least for a while, the zoning map could help ensure that the escape to the suburbs would not mean again facing the problems that movers intended to leave behind.

Today, many wealthier suburbs continue to resist the pressure to seek regional solutions to the highly complex transportation, housing, employment, taxation, and environmental problems facing metropolitan areas. That they can do so is in many ways a product of the Taft Court's generous indulgence of local governance. While some states have used carrots and sticks to force all metropolitan players to come to the table, one need only study rapid transit maps, standardized test scores, real estate taxation rates, and, of course, zoning maps to see that many suburbs have chosen to go their own way, often to the detriment of the central city. Moreover, while *Euclid v. Ambler* helped pave the way for judicial acceptance of environmental regulation passed in support of the public interest, it has also insulated from legal challenge local, self-interested efforts to exclude windmill farms and state-of-the-art waste treatment and disposal facilities.

In the 1980s, there was some hope that, with the growing popularity of regional and statewide planning (as opposed to almost total local control), parochialism was at last on the wane. Even in the pages of Justice Sutherland's opinion one can find a warning that local governments cannot push their newfound self-determination too far: "It is not meant by this, however, to exclude the possibility of cases where the general public interest would so far outweigh the interest of the municipality that the municipality would not be allowed to stand in the way." As it turns out, however, state and federal courts for the most part have ignored this Euclidean caveat.

There are other telling signs that, despite some optimism a few decades ago, parochialism is alive and thriving in the area of land-use regulation. First, growth control or growth management ordinances continue to attract the attention of local government officials because, depending on one's outlook, they either provide a necessary time out for areas experiencing intense growth pressures in order to develop wise, comprehensive plans to protect the environment and preserve a small-town quality of life, or they serve as an effective method that insiders use to keep out lower-income newcomers whose mere presence might reduce existing property values. The likelihood that the second motivation is a significant factor increases when the no- or slow-growth scheme is effected through "ballot-box zoning" — referenda and initiatives that enable the local citizenry to stand up to developers when their elected officials are perceived to be too malleable.

Second, despite the growing number of critics who decry suburban sprawl and the increasing isolation and impoverishment of the inner city, new, self-governed edge cities are proliferating throughout the country. Joel Garreau, who popularized the term in his 1988 book, *Edge City: Life on the New Frontier*, has described the phenomenon this way:

> Our new city centers are tied together not by locomotives and subways, but by jetways, freeways, and rooftop satellite dishes thirty feet across. Their characteristic monument is not a horse-mounted hero, but the atria reaching for the sun and shielding trees perpetually in leaf at the cores of corporate headquarters, fitness centers, and shopping plazas. These new urban areas are marked not by the penthouses of the old urban rich or the tenements of the old urban poor. Instead, their landmark structure is the celebrated single-family detached dwelling, the suburban home with grass all around that made America the best-housed civilization the world has ever known.

There are no significant disincentives — legal, economic, or social — to the increased popularity of these beltway behemoths that grow *at the expense of*, not in concert with, the older urban centers in the region — central cities and aged suburbs alike.

Third, the New Jersey Supreme Court's mandate in the *Mount Laurel* litigation, requiring individual localities to meet their regional obligations to provide their fair share of affordable housing, has spawned too few imitations. Even in the Garden State, the Fair Housing Act allows suburban communities to opt out of up to half of their fair share by agreeing to pay for housing in the inner city. In providing this avenue of "cooperation," state lawmakers have enabled the continuation of the notion that cities and their suburbs are "separate kingdoms" whose destinies are distinct, if not *de facto*, then at least *de jure*.

Fourth, despite a great deal of rhetoric and numerous supporting studies over the last few decades, there have been no significant steps taken toward effective and widespread regional planning and governance. The most prominent advocate for reconceptualizing the American city, David Rusk, has noted that "reversing the fragmentation of urban areas is an essential step in ending severe racial and economic segregation." The solution—reunifying city and suburb—though easy to articulate, has proved quite difficult to implement. This reality is in no small way attributable to popular resistance to metropolitan-wide solutions and to some very real legal barriers, not the least of which is the Euclidean legacy of local control over planning and zoning decision making.

Implementing Aesthetics-Based Controls

The value of the final seed planted in *Euclid v. Ambler* is truly in the eye of the beholder. That aesthetics underlie zoning and its judicial approval is undeniable. Despite subsequent, official denials by proponents of zoning, aesthetic sensibility originally was an important component of height, area, and use controls. For every planner who attempted to rationalize the work of the profession by noting "The Sheer Cost of Ugliness" (the title of an address to the Sixteenth National Conference on City Planning in 1924), there was another who would assert that beauty was good in and of itself:

The object of the City Planning Conference, as I understand it, is not only to promote cities and towns which shall be more convenient for business and for traffic, but also to promote cities and towns which shall be more beautiful places in which to live. . . . We must consider for children not only plenty of air and plenty of light and playgrounds, but we must consider also beautiful surroundings in which they shall grow up.

The speaker was Mrs. W. L. Lawton of Glens Falls, New York, who in 1926 was the chair of the National Committee for Restriction of Outdoor Advertising.

Ambler's legal counsel, Newton D. Baker, summarized the point in an argument designed to contrast such unsupportable subjectivity with the weighty demands made by the Due Process Clause. "Even if the world could agree by unanimous consent upon what is beautiful and desirable," he wrote, "it could not, under our constitutional theory, enforce its decision by prohibiting a land owner, who refuses to accept the world's view of beauty, from making otherwise safe and innocent uses of his land." This carefully crafted argument missed its mark, however, as the majority in *Euclid v. Ambler* was less concerned about the rights of the landowner than about the perception that, in the words of the opinion, "the coming of the apartment is followed by others, interfering by their height and bulk with the free circulation of air and monopolizing the rays of the sun which otherwise would fall upon the smaller homes."

During the early decades of judicially approved land-use planning and zoning, courts reasoned that, while aesthetics alone could not serve as the sole basis for approving a regulation on the use of land, as long as the challenged regulation promoted the legitimate police power goals of health, safety, morals, and general welfare, it would survive judicial scrutiny. Lawmakers in the early 1970s, in a move consistent with the growing environmental movement, created regulatory schemes designed to eliminate visual pollution, often with court approval. By the end of the twentieth century, it appeared that a new majority of states had approved of land-use regulations based on aesthetics alone. Moreover, the U.S. Supreme Court, in a series of cases involving challenges to urban renewal (*Berman v. Parker* in 1954), historic preservation (*Penn Central Transportation Co. v. New York City* in 1978), and billboard and sign regulation (*Metromedia, Inc.*

v. City of San Diego in 1981) cast its important vote in favor of aesthetics-based controls.

By 1984, some more liberal members of the Court were voicing their concern that aesthetics could be a cloak for stifling free speech. That year, in *Members of City Council of Los Angeles v. Taxpayers for Vincent*, the majority held that a city ordinance prohibiting the posting of signs on public property did not violate the first amendment rights of a group of supporters for a political candidate. Justice William Brennan, joined by Thurgood Marshall and Harry Blackmun, dissented, opining that "the Court's lenient approach towards the restriction of speech for reasons of aesthetics threatens seriously to undermine the protections of the First Amendment. . . . The City of Los Angeles has not shown that its interest in eliminating 'visual clutter' justifies its restriction of appellees' ability to communicate with the local electorate." Some troubling notions were walking into the door that was opened by *Euclid v. Ambler*.

Even advocates of aesthetic regulations have conceded that some excesses and missteps have plagued this area. John Costonis has observed that "countless aesthetics initiatives have streamed through the floodgates that judges have unlocked. Many of these initiatives are superb, both in concept and administration. Others have been neither, rendering legal aesthetics vulnerable to the Dump Aesthetics critique." Particularly troubling are the developments in the areas of historic preservation and adult use that imperil fundamental First Amendment rights.

Emboldened by their victory in *Penn Central*, preservationists have tightened the restrictions placed on buildings and sites that are deemed architecturally, historically, or culturally significant. In the great majority of cases public officials have proceeded in a manner respectful of vested property and other rights. Nevertheless, there are some disturbing exceptions. The politically and culturally charged struggle over the plans of St. Bartholomew's Episcopal Church to replace its community building in New York City with a massive office tower dragged out over a decade, ending with the Supreme Court's refusal in 1991 to overturn the federal appellate court's decision that neither an illegal taking nor a violation of free exercise of religion protections had occurred. A year later the First

Covenant Church of Seattle was more successful in its challenge to landmark designation, although it took more than a dozen years, two trips to the state supreme court, and a detour to the U.S. Supreme Court to prevail on its free exercise claim. Similarly, in 1993 the supreme court of Pennsylvania held that the Philadelphia Historical Commission, in designating the *interior* of the historic Boyd Theater as historically and architecturally significant, had overstepped its legal bounds.

A historic preservation conflict pitting the city of Boerne, Texas, against the Catholic Archbishop of San Antonio sent reverberations through America's houses of worship, local governments, state legislatures, Congress, and the White House. In *City of Boerne v. Flores* (1997), a splintered Supreme Court struck down parts of the Religious Freedom Restoration Act (RFRA), a federal statute designed to provide even greater protections than the Supreme Court afforded individuals when government at any level — federal, state, or local — substantially burdens the free exercise of religion. Boerne officials, claiming that the St. Peter Catholic Church was located in a historic district, denied the archbishop's application to enlarge the building to accommodate a growing parish population. He sued in federal district court claiming that the city had violated the strong protections afforded by RFRA, but the lower court found that Congress had exceeded its authority in passing the statute. The federal appeals court reversed, but the Supreme Court majority agreed with the district court. By forcing states and localities to come up with a "compelling governmental interest" for burdening free exercise and to use the "least restrictive means" to further that interest, Congress had stepped over the line between legislatively enforcing the provisions of the Free Exercise Clause of the First Amendment and altering the clause's meaning, which was the judiciary's function.

The archbishop and preservationists won this battle, but the war is still in doubt. Congress and the president renewed their efforts to provide enhanced free exercise protections in two key areas by passing the Religious Land Use and Institutionalized Persons Act of 2000. RLUIPA singles out violations of religious freedom by prison officials and by land-use regulators enforcing zoning, historic preservation, and related controls. The new statute is anti-Euclidean in the sense that local governments are given much less deference than in the typical landowner challenge to zoning. RLUIPA has in some cases proved to be a powerful weapon against local government officials when they attempt to satisfy the subjective desires and unwarranted prejudices of landowners who are disturbed by the presence of churches, temples, synagogues, and mosques in their neighborhoods or communities. According to critics, in some instances RLUIPA has been abused by religious groups that attempt to invoke the protections of the act for land development activities that are only marginally related to core religious practices and values.

Aesthetics-based land-use regulations have raised concerns in other First Amendment contexts as well. When, for example, officials in a Washington city sought to concentrate adult theatres rather than disperse them throughout the city, the Supreme Court, in *City of Renton v. Playtime Theatres, Inc.* (1986), held that the First Amendment's free speech protections did not obligate the city to tailor its regulatory scheme to the meet the city's specific circumstances:

> We hold that Renton was entitled to rely on the experiences of Seattle and other cities . . . in enacting its adult theater zoning ordinance. The First Amendment does not require a city, before enacting such an ordinance, to conduct new studies or produce evidence independent of that already generated by other cities, so long as whatever evidence the city relies upon is reasonably believed to be relevant to the problem that the city addresses.

It is not hard to see how *Euclid v. Ambler* inspired this one-size-fits-all approach to land-use controls, given the village's reliance on New York's zoning study and the popularity in cities large and small of the Standard State Zoning Enabling Act circulated by the Commerce Department in the 1920s. The deference in the *Renton* case resembles that found in the typical Euclidean zoning case, one that involves no serious allegation that landowner's fundamental rights have been violated.

Eight years after the *Renton* decision, the Court, troubled by a Missouri city's widespread regulation of residential signs, reacted with a finding that was protective of a landowner's free speech rights. In *City of Ladue v. Gilleo* (1994), the city's aesthetic goals were apparent in the sign ordinance's "Declaration of Findings, Policies, Interests, and Purposes." The local regulators, combining aesthetics with more traditional police power concerns, complained there that the

> proliferation of an unlimited number of signs in private, residential, commercial, industrial, and public areas of the City of Ladue would create ugliness, visual blight and clutter, tarnish the natural beauty of the landscape as well as the residential and commercial architecture, impair property values, substantially impinge upon the privacy and special ambience of the community, and may cause safety and traffic hazards to motorists, pedestrians, and children.

Margaret P. Gilleo violated the ordinance by posting a sign in a second-story window of her house; the offending display—measuring eight-and-one-half inches by eleven inches—read, "For Peace in the Gulf."

The *Ladue* Court, treading carefully on already unsteady jurisprudential terrain, declared that the city had overstepped the bounds set by the First Amendment. While the justices conceded the validity of Ladue's "interest in minimizing visual clutter," they were seriously troubled that the city "almost completely foreclosed a venerable means of communication that is both unique and important. It has totally foreclosed that medium to political, religious, or personal messages." The Court could not have been surprised that cities such as Ladue would have embarked on such zealous campaigns in the name of beauty, given the imprimatur the justices had placed on a wide range of aesthetic-based regulation of land.

Zoning, much like the metropolitan areas that continue to use the device as a central component of its land-use regulatory regime, has continued to evolve since its origins during the opening decades of the twentieth century. Hindsight makes it appear that many of the eventual abuses of zoning were not only inevitable but also intentional. The historical record, however, instructs us that this appearance is deceiving. While it is true that many early advocates of zoning may have placed too much trust in the skills of experts and the findings of various studies and reports, there is little if any evidence that the campaign for zoning was an organized effort designed to achieve either (1) centralized, government planning in opposition to private property rights or (2) the isolation and exclusion of nonpropertied classes. In the Village of Euclid, as in many of the nation's cities and towns over the past one hundred years, zoning was a good-faith, though certainly imperfect, effort to improve the quality of life for current residents and their future residential, commercial, and industrial neighbors.

Return to Euclid

The main actors in the *Euclid v. Ambler* drama have long since parted this world. D. C. Westenhaver, who died of heart disease at age sixty-three in 1928, was the first to pass. Even the *New York Times* reported his death, taking note of his expertise in patent law and participation in the Debs prosecution.

Today Alfred Bettman lives on in the hearts of countless planners. Many have given credit for the Supreme Court victory to the force of Bettman's arguments concerning the nuisance prevention and aesthetic preservation character of zoning. It is not hard spot these elements in Justice Sutherland's careful, well-reasoned opinion. With the passage of time, the Bettman legend has grown. For example, lawyer and planner Timothy Fluck's sixtieth anniversary essay on the case closes thus: "few individuals could have personified the American city planning movement in the Court's eyes as ably as Alfred Bettman." Like Baker, Bettman's devotion to public service took him to Washington, D.C., where he served as an assistant attorney general in the Department of Justice. A true devotee of planning, Bettman was a key figure in the drafting of the Standard City Planning Enabling Act, which the Commerce Department published in 1928. He chaired Cincinnati's official planning commission from 1930 until his death in 1945. Although his public service was not limited to the field of planning, it is his most enduring legacy.

Baker's main legacy is the large and highly respected firm that still bears his name — Baker Hostetler — with hundreds of lawyers in Cleveland, other American cities, and in foreign countries. Among political junkies, he will also be remembered for the fact that in 1932 he almost received the Democratic nomination for president. A sharp opponent of isolationism before and after World War I, Baker fought valiantly, though fruitlessly, for American membership in the League of Nations and was appointed by President Calvin Coolidge to the Permanent Court of Arbitration at The Hague. His urban reform efforts, contributions to public charities, and public service are widely recognized to this day. But his work on behalf of two of his most important clients—the Van Sweringen brothers—has faded from American memory. Within five years of the dedication of the grand Cleveland Union Terminal in June 1930, the Van Sweringens' vast railroad empire began to collapse, leading to a national scandal of Enron proportions. Like Baker, who died in 1937, the two brothers, who died in 1935 and 1936, were buried in Cleveland's Lake View Cemetery.

Metzenbaum's shadow, in contrast with Bettman's and Baker's, is much less in evidence today. The time and energy he expended in refuting Baker's characterizations of the village's actual and potential land uses and of the ordinance's effects on Ambler's parcel appear to have been wasted, until we realize that what Sutherland and his fellow justices said about value was irrelevant to the outcome of the case. The same cannot be said for two other arguments raised in the village's three briefs: first, that the Court has traditionally been deferential to state and local police power regulations, and second, that constitutional law is adaptable to changing conditions.

Four years after the village's victory, Metzenbaum published the first volume of his treatise, *The Law of Zoning*, in no small part a rendition of his "four years of unbroken effort" culminating in the opinion in *Euclid v. Ambler*. Although he never again appeared before the Supreme Court, Metzenbaum would be identified with zoning and planning law for the remainder of his life, as he continued his general practice in Cleveland (in the 1010 Euclid Building), served three terms as a member of the Cleveland School Board and of the Ohio Senate (his cousin Howard would serve in that state body and in the U.S. Senate), and devoted himself unwaveringly to the memory of his wife, Bessie.

That devotion appears to hold the keys to the melancholy that plagued Metzenbaum for decades and to his indefatigable advocacy in the *Euclid* case. Shortly after Metzenbaum's death on December 31, 1960 (fifty-four years to the day after his wedding), a column appeared in the *Cleveland Plain Dealer* titled "Brilliant Metzenbaum Led Melancholy Life." The columnist, a long-time observer of political life in the city and state, recalled his first interview with the local attorney:

> He told me of his life sadness, the death of his young wife, his devotion to her mausoleum, his sense of wretchedness at everything he did no matter how materially successful it might turn out. A part of his time, his speech was broken with anguish, and tears came several times.

A few years later, after the Supreme Court announced its decision in *Euclid*, the two men met again. Metzenbaum looked "perturbed as ever, but actually with a heart brimming over his triumph. For he had been terrified . . . to go up against Mr. Baker, who by then was believed infallible in any lawsuit—his personal guiding star, to boot." That bittersweet moment stood out as an exception, however, in Metzenbaum's long, disconsolate life.

Bessie Benner Metzenbaum, who died suddenly in 1920 during a trip to Florida, inspired two lasting legacies. The first—the association of Euclid with the history and legitimacy of American zoning—can be traced to her widower's affection for the village that was the young couple's home during their short life together and for the cause of providing "shelter and protection" for the "American home." Indeed, the dedication for *The Law of Zoning* reads, "To the memory of one whose devoted care brought back the strength to do this work."

The second legacy, Bessie Benner Metzenbaum Park, sits on the site of a farm in Chester Township, Geauga County, Ohio. In 1948, Metzenbaum deeded a parcel, which he had discovered while taking a long ride during one of his many sleepless nights, to the Bessie Benner Metzenbaum Foundation and, according to Jay Abercrombie's guidebook for the Western Reserve, the widower "undertook his latest crusade with characteristic fervor":

> He would arrive at the Chester property at 3 or 4, morning after morning, working on the farm before going to his Cleveland office by 9 AM. Many evenings were also spent on the project. His plan was to establish a facility for the use of deprived or handicapped children "regardless of race, color or creed, and without

cost to such children." The foundation established a school for children and later a sheltered workshop for handicapped adults.

In 1991, the foundation gave sixty-five acres to the county's park district, allowing pubic access to the park and its wheelchair-accessible trail.

Metzenbaum's melancholy ended on New Year's Eve, 1960, when he suffered a heart attack while visiting Bessie's mausoleum at Lake View Cemetery. Nature again had played a fateful role in Metzenbaum's life story, for according to the obituary in the *New York Times*, "police said his car was stuck in snow and [Metzenbaum] may have over-exerted himself trying to push it free." At the memorial service, Rabbi Philip Horowitz noted the link between the lawyer's activism and the memory of his wife:

He was uncompromising and incorruptible. He fought hard and sometimes bitterly for what he believed in.

If our suburbs are more beautiful, we owe that in part to him. His work affected thousands of schoolchildren. We remember him for his passionate devotion to social justice.

He converted his 40 years of idolizing his wife into a life of benefaction.

Two or three times a week, for four decades, Metzenbaum visited the cemetery. Along with Bessie's ashes, the mausoleum contained small living quarters and a rocking chair and was supplied with electrical power. Lake View Cemetery, where James Metzenbaum joined his bride in 1961, sits on the eastern side of the city, at 12316 Euclid Avenue, directly in the path of urban sprawl between central city Cleveland and Euclid.

The history of Euclid indicates that, in the long run, no municipality is an island. Sixteen square miles of predominantly agricultural land when it was incorporated in 1903, the Village of Euclid was a relatively new government unit when its officials began studying zoning. Through the village ran Euclid Avenue, the continuation of a street in Cleveland that once boasted a collection of the nation's grandest mansions, but that in the 1920s was in decline, like many of the nation's grand avenues. Industry was already at the back door, as the Cleveland Tractor Company plant had set up business adjoining the Nickel Plate Road in the village.

In the municipality immortalized by the term "Euclidean," zoning alone could not keep the perceived "evils" of neighboring Cleveland at bay—not its ethnic residents and not its industry. According to the 2000 Census, of the 52,000 residents of Euclid, more than 4,000 listed their ancestry as Slovene, 3,000 as Polish, 5,000 as Italian, and more than 1,000 as Slovak, Hungarian, or Croatian. More than 16,000 of the residents in 2000 were listed as Black or African American.

The Ambler Realty site itself has also undergone significant changes since 1926. Efforts to protect the Ambler parcel from industrial intrusion proved fruitless in the face of global military conflict. During World War II, the federal government acquired the Ambler Realty site in order to construct a plant to produce aircraft engines and landing gear. Many of the eastern European immigrants who settled in Euclid during this period were attracted by the boom in industry during and in the years following the war.

When peace arrived, General Motors acquired the facility, converting it into a Fisher Body Division auto-assembly plant. The assembly plant operated from 1948 to 1970, after which the facility turned out seats and trim in what was then called the Inland Fisher Guide Plant. In December 1992, GM officials announced that the plant would be mothballed in 1994, as part of the company's efforts to downsize in order to increase profits, but the plant closing took place a year earlier than originally planned. In March 1996, the 1 million-square-foot industrial complex was purchased for $2.5 million by a St. Louis investment company, which planned to redevelop the property as an industrial complex with multiple tenants. These plans fit in with the character of the neighborhood at the time—a blend of residential, commercial, and industrial uses that included bungalows and high-rise apartments. Within four years, the property changed hands two more times—first to a California industrial building recycler, then to a major tenant of the building, a warehousing and logistics company that paid $10 million for the property and its aging structures.

Eighty years after the decision in *Euclid v. Ambler*, the locus of the dispute – the former GM plant at 20001 Euclid Avenue – would be a multiuse facility that housed the Euclid Sports Plant, a 60,000-square-foot sports complex in which teams and individuals could practice and compete; HGR Industrial Surplus, which featured a 10-acre showroom with over 70,000 items in stock; a warehouse and distribution facilty operated by Handl-it Inc.; and the Euclid Police Department's Southwest Office.

Even in a postindustrial economy, nearly one-quarter of the employment in 1990s Euclid was in manufacturing, supported in part by tax concessions and enterprise zone incentives. If, as some have posited, the Supreme Court majority coalesced around the effort to preserve private property from an invasion of "new immigrants," the strategy has backfired badly. By century's end, the ethnically diverse population in search of the Euclidean ideal – detached, single-family housing – had little to choose from, as more than half of Euclid's residential single-family housing stock consisted of 1950s bungalows situated on small parcels. With very few available homes in the $125,000-plus price range, planners puzzled over ways to keep upwardly mobile families from leaving.

The residents of Euclid were aware of their rich historical heritage. In 1989, the American Institute of Certified Planners recognized the city as a planning landmark. Five years later, the city marked its origins by dedicating Surveyors' Park – a green space, featuring a circular reflecting pond, in the center of Euclid's retail district.

Debates over Euclidean zoning remain heated in the twentieth century. In 2001 Professor Gerald Korngold observed on the seventy-fifth anniversary of the holding that the "milestone Supreme Court decision" in *Euclid v. Ambler* "has had a profound effect on American life and jurisprudence. The decision provided the constitutional foundation for an explosive growth in modern zoning, subdivision controls, and other governmental land-use regulation that has transformed the organization and development of land and communities." Many commentators have bemoaned this "profound effect." There are those who advocate wrenching local planning and zoning decision making from the hands of local government officials. Skeptical about the abilities of these local officials to plan wisely, to resist bribes and other forms of corruption, and to plan with the best interests of the region in mind, this group of critics seeks to lodge zoning functions at the state level.

Another volley of criticism has been lobbed by the New Urbanists, a loosely connected movement of architects, planners, and developers who list among their goals "the restoration of existing urban centers and towns within coherent metropolitan regions, the reconfiguration of sprawling suburbs into communities of real neighborhoods and diverse districts, the conservation of natural environments, and the preservation of our built legacy." The segregation of commercial and residential uses by the typical Euclidean zoning ordinance is a special target of some of the movement's most outspoken advocates. One leading book on the subject, *Suburban Nation: The Rise of Sprawl and the Decline of the American Dream*, has lodged this complaint:

> If our communities are to recover from sprawl, they need both new regulations and a new regulatory environment. Existing zoning ordinances — typically outdated, overcomplicated, and vulnerable to influence peddling — are often discredited but rarely discarded. The flaws of these ordinances are too many to mention here, but can be gleaned through even cursory reading. Most need radical restructuring just to open the door for traditional development.

Advocates of the somewhat nebulous concept called "smart growth," which is essentially a multipronged attack on suburban and exurban sprawl and an effort to update land-use controls, are also highly critical of traditional, Euclidean zoning and its segregation of land uses.

In order to contrast their novel ideas with ideas from the distant and outmoded past, many New Urbanists and some Smart Growth advocates simply ignore post-Euclidean modifications that were developed to make zoning more flexible beginning in the 1960s, such as transferable development rights, mixed-use zoning, and conditional and performance zoning. While the basic criticism of 1920s-style height, area, and use zoning ordinances is a valid one, the claim that eliminating the vestiges of Euclidean zoning would help reduce sprawl suffers from two weaknesses. First, although Euclidean deference to local control was a significant enabler of communities that refused to engage in regional planning, it took much more than zoning to create the late twentieth-century version of sprawl. Second, many New Urbanist communities have been built at the outer boundaries of metropolitan areas, leapfrogging over available land closer to urban neighborhoods. Most important, while Euclidean zoning may be an obstacle to the good life in the eyes of New Urbanists and Smart Growth proponents, these critics would not be able to realize their vision without "Euclidean" deference by the judiciary.

A third group of critics believes that the *Euclid v. Ambler* problem lies with government regulation per se. They would rather leave it up to the market to determine development patterns, relying on private land-use controls and common-law concepts such as private nuisance to prevent and resolve disputes over discordant uses of land. Taking this path would require a vast rewriting of state and local laws, given the fact that zoning is now authorized in every state and that there are zoning ordinances of one kind or another in every major city except Houston (a city that has an alternative package of public and private regulations). Of course, if the Supreme Court reversed the central holding of *Euclid v. Ambler* and recognized that zoning actually did deprive landowners of their property without due process of law, or, in the alternative, took their property without just compensation, then that vast rewriting of laws would become a legal necessity.

Beginning in the late 1970s, there has been an ample amount of legal scholarship advocating such a move, building upon Justice Holmes's notion that a regulation that goes "too far" can amount to a taking, a taking that would be unconstitutional without compensation. There have even been a few U.S. Supreme Court decisions, most notably *Lucas v. South Carolina Coastal Council* (1992), in which the justices have determined that an unconstitutional "regulatory taking" has occurred. This issue remains a hotly contested one in state and federal courts, with courts struggling mightily, as did the Court in *Euclid v. Ambler*, to balance private rights with public needs.

On June 23, 2005, the American public's attention was drawn to the issue of private property rights protection when the Court announced its holding in *Kelo v. City of New London*. To many lawyers and legal commentators, this appeared to be a fairly routine case in which homeowners, who were offered fair market value for their properties, were told that they would not be able to stand in the way of a large redevelopment project that promised to increase employment and increase tax revenues in a distressed Connecticut city. To many in the media and to private property rights advocates, the message of *Kelo* was that all American homes were endangered by government interference. The majority opinion, which emphasized that the city was acting in accordance with a "comprehensive redevelopment plan," cited *Euclid v. Ambler* in the middle of the following supportive sentence: "with other exercises in urban planning and development, the City is endeavoring to coordinate a variety of commercial, residential, and recreational uses of land, with the hope that they will form a whole greater than the sum of its parts." This was not enough to assuage the concerns of the dissenters, who thought that the city had crossed the line of permissible conduct.

The decision in *Kelo* highlighted the tension inherent in government regulation of property, particularly land. In *Euclid*, the majority, citing the widespread expert opinion in support of zoning, refused to elevate the protection of private property rights to such a high degree that public officials would have a hard time demonstrating their necessity, or even reasonableness. Instead, the Court decided to respect the police power that, under our constitutional structure, is reserved to states and localities, by placing the burden on the landowner to show that the regulator was acting in an unreasonable or arbitrary manner. If not for that key 1926 decision, most Americans would not be living in "zoned" cities. Moreover, unless the judicial shift that occurred in the late 1930s in favor of New Deal regulation would have reversed such an antizoning holding, there is a good chance that we would not have seen the full panoply of modern environmental regulations on the federal, state, and local levels. After all, many of those regulations, such as laws protecting wetlands, beaches, and endangered species, have an effect on many landowners' abilities to maximize the profit from "full" development of their properties.

Without a long-standing decision such as *Euclid v. Ambler* on the books instructing that there is no fundamental constitutional right to the speculative value of land, would these and other programs have survived the inevitable legal challenge that followed their enactment? Thanks to the authoritativeness of Justice Sutherland's opinion for the Court in *Euclid v. Ambler* and to the other zoning decisions from the 1920s, there is no need to answer this question today. Thanks to the highly volatile world of urban and suburban land development, and to the evolving nature of American constitutional law, change is just one cry of "Oyez! Oyez! Oyez!" away.

Lucas v. South Carolina Coastal Council, 505 U.S. 1003 (1992)

McCardle v. Indianapolis Water Co., 272 U.S. 400 (1926)

Members of City Council of Los Angeles v. Taxpayers for Vincent, 466 U.S. 789 (1984)

Metromedia, Inc. v. City of San Diego, 453 U.S. 490 (1981)

Michigan v. Wisconsin, 272 U.S. 398 (1926)

Muller v. Oregon, 208 U.S. 412 (1908)

Nectow v. City of Cambridge, 277 U.S. 183 (1928)

New York ex rel. Rosevale Realty Co. v. Kleinert, 268 U.S. 646 (1925)

Norway Plains Co. v. Boston & Maine Railroad, 67 Mass. 263 (1854)

Penn Central Transportation Co. v. New York City, 438 U.S. 104 (1978)

Pennsylvania Coal Co. v. Mahon, 260 U.S. 393 (1922)

Powell v. Alabama, 287 U.S. 45 (1932)

Pritz v. Messer, 112 Ohio St. 628, 149 N.E. 30 (1925).

Rector, Wardens, & Members of Vestry of St. Bartholomew's Church v. City of New York, 914 F.2d 348 (2d Cir. 1990), *cert. denied, Committee to Oppose Sale of Saint Bartholomew's Church, Inc. v. Rector, Wardens, & Members of the Vestry of Saint Bartholomew's Church*, 499 U.S. 905 (1991)

Russell v. Harpel, 1900 Ohio Misc. LEXIS 192, 10 Ohio Cir. Dec. 732 (1900)

Schechter Poultry Corp. v. United States, 295 U.S. 495 (1935)

Second Church of Christ, Scientist v. LePrevost, 35 N.E. 2d 1015 (Ohio Ct. App. 1941)

Shelley v. Kraemer, 334 U.S. 1 (1948)

Soon Hing v. Crowley, 113 U.S. 703 (1885)

Southern Burlington County N.A.A.C.P. v. Township of Mount Laurel, 336 A.2d 713 (N.J. 1975)

Southern Pacific Co. v. United States, 272 U.S. 445 (1926)

State ex rel. Ohio Hair Products Co. v. Rendigs, 98 Ohio St. 251, 120 N.E. 836 (1918)

State ex rel. Euclid-Doan Building Co. v. Cunningham, 97 Ohio St. 130, 119 N.E. 361 (1918)

State ex rel. Morris v. East Cleveland, 31 Ohio Dec. 98 (1919), on rehearing at 22 Ohio N.P. (n.s.) (1919)

State v. Durant, 2 Ohio L. Abs. 75 (1923)

Thomas Cusack Co. v. City of Chicago, 242 U.S. 526 (1917)

United Artists' Theater Circuit v. City of Philadelphia, 635 A.2d 612 (Pa. 1993)

United States v. New York Central Railroad Co., 272 U.S. 457 (1926)

United States v. One Ford Coupe Automobile, 272 U.S. 321 (1926)

Van Oster v. Kansas, 272 U.S. 465 (1926)

Village of Euclid v. Ambler Realty Co., 272 U.S. 365 (1926)

Village of University Heights v. Cleveland Jewish Orphans' Home, 20 F.2d 743 (6th Cir. 1927)

Welch v. Swazey, 214 U.S. 91 (1909)
Yankton Sioux Tribe v. United States, 272 U.S. 351 (1926)
Yick Wo v. Hopkins, 118 U.S. 356 (1886)
Zahn v. Board of Public Works, 274 U.S. 325 (1927)

CHRONOLOGY

July 22, 1796	Moses Cleaveland and his survey party arrive at the mouth of Cuyahoga River, the site of modern-day Cleveland, Ohio.
1809	Euclid Township is incorporated.
May 10, 1886	U.S. Supreme Court, in *Yick Wo v. Hopkins*, finds that San Francisco officials enforcing an ordinance regulating public laundries discriminated against the Chinese in violation of the Equal Protection Clause of the U.S. Constitution.
1893	Chicago hosts the World's Columbian Exposition, featuring the influential architecture of the "White City."
1902	Daniel Burnham, a central figure in the 1893 Exposition, is named to Cleveland's Group Plan Commission.
1903	Village of Euclid is incorporated.
1905	The Van Sweringen brothers begin acquiring land in the Cleveland suburb of Shaker Heights.
1909	The First National Conference of City Planning convenes in Washington, D.C.
1911	Ambler Realty Company purchases undeveloped parcel in Euclid, located between the Nickel Plate Road and Euclid Avenue.
December 23, 1913	The New York City Height of Buildings Commission issues its influential report.
1915	Ohio enacts municipal planning legislation.
February 1916	President Woodrow Wilson names Newton D. Baker Secretary of War.
July 1916	The New York City Board of Estimate adopts the nation's first comprehensive zoning ordinance.
1916	The Van Sweringen brothers purchase a majority interest in the Nickel Plate Road.
1916	D. C. Westenhaver is appointed as a judge on the U.S. District Court for the Northern District of Ohio.

November 5, 1917	U.S. Supreme Court declares Louisville, Kentucky's racial zoning ordinance unconstitutional in *Buchanan v. Warley*.
1918	Judge Westenhaver sentences Eugene V. Debs to a ten-year prison sentence for violating the Espionage Act of 1917.
May 1, 1919	May Day Riots erupt in Cleveland.
May 13, 1920	Ohio legislature adopts zoning enabling legislation.
1921	Baker founds the Cleveland law firm of Baker, Hostetler & Sidlo.
September 1922	The U.S. Department of Commerce circulates thousands of copies of the preliminary version of its Standard Zoning Enabling Act (SZEA).
May 1922	Euclid's planning commission begins studying zoning and drafts its first ordinance.
November 13, 1922	The Village Council of Euclid adopts Ordinance 2812, the municipality's first zoning ordinance.
April 1923	Several Euclid landowners execute expense underwriting agreement with Baker to fund legal challenges to zoning.
May 5, 1923	Ambler Realty files a complaint in federal district court challenging Euclid's Ordinance 2812.
June 11, 1923	The Village of Euclid adopts three landowner-friendly amendments to its original zoning ordinance.
December 1923	Lawyers for both sides conduct depositions in Cleveland.
January 14, 1924	Federal District Judge Westenhaver rules in the landowner's favor in *Ambler Realty Co. v. Village of Euclid*.
May 1924	The U.S. Department of Commerce issues a final version of the SZEA (revised in 1926).
January 27, 1926	The first oral argument before the U.S. Supreme Court is heard in *Euclid v. Ambler*.
March 1, 1926	The Supreme Court announces that *Euclid v. Ambler* will be reargued in October, 1926.
October 12, 1926	The second oral argument is heard in *Euclid v. Ambler*.

November 22, 1926	The Supreme Court announces its holding in the Village's favor in *Euclid v. Ambler*.
May 14, 1928	In *Nectow v. City of Cambridge*, the Supreme Court upholds a landowner's constitutional challenge to zoning as applied to his property.
1928	The U.S. Department of Commerce publishes its Standard City Planning Enabling Act.
1930	James Metzenbaum publishes the first edition of *The Law of Zoning*.
1941	The federal government opens a manufacturing facility on the Ambler Realty site for the production of aircraft engines and landing gear (in 1947, General Motors took over the installation and converted it into an auto assembly plant).
May 3, 1948	The U.S. Supreme Court, in *Shelley v. Kraemer*, declares enforcement of racially restrictive, private covenants in deeds to be violation of Equal Protection Clause.
December 31, 1960	Metzenbaum dies while visiting his wife's mausoleum at Cleveland's Lake View Cemetery.
March 24, 1975	In *Southern Burlington County N.A.A.C.P. v. Township of Mount Laurel*, the Supreme Court of New Jersey declares exclusionary zoning invalid under its state constitution.
1992	General Motors announces the mothballing of its Fisher Guide facility in Euclid (the plant, which since 1970 had been used to produce automobile trim, was closed in 1993).

BIBLIOGRAPHICAL ESSAY

Note from the Series Editors: The following bibliographical essay contains the primary and secondary sources the author consulted for this volume. We have asked all authors in the series to omit formal citations in order to make our volumes more readable, inexpensive, and appealing for students and general readers.

The Transcript of Record for *Euclid v. Ambler*, along with seven briefs (by the parties and *amici*) are available in the electronic database *The Making of Modern Law: U.S. Supreme Court Records and Briefs, 1832–1978* (Thomson West). The case file in the National Archives contains Supreme Court documents and correspondence between the clerk's office and counsel. Many of the briefs have also been published in Volume 24 of *Landmark Briefs and Arguments of the Supreme Court of the United States: Constitutional Law* (Arlington, Va.: University Publications of Virginia, 1975). The William Howard Taft Papers (available in microfilm) contain relevant correspondence to and from George Sutherland, Alfred Bettman, and James Metzenbaum. The archives of Baker Hostetler's Cleveland office contain some of the materials produced and used by Newton Baker in the district court and in the Supreme Court. Arthur V. N. Brooks, a former partner in the firm, has assembled and preserved correspondence and other important documents related to the case. Newspaper coverage of the events described in the book can be found in the *Christian Science Monitor, Cleveland Plain Dealer, Cleveland Press and News, Crain's Cleveland Business, New York Times, Wall Street Journal,* and *Washington Post.*

Because *Euclid v. Ambler* was and remains the central case in American land-use regulation and zoning law, there have been many treatments of the case and its history in history, law, and planning publications. The classic and enduring treatment of the early history of zoning is Seymour I. Toll, *Zoned American* (New York: Grossman Publishers, 1969). Also helpful on New York City's early zoning experiment is Raphaël Fischler, "The Metropolitan Dimension of Early Zoning: Revisiting the 1916 New York City Ordinance," 64 *Journal of the American Planning Association* 170 (1998). The reader can find a valuable collection of essays in Charles M. Haar and Jerold S. Kayden, editors, *Zoning and the American Dream: Promises Still to Keep* (Chicago: Planners Press, 1989). In addition to my own contribution, "The Prescience and Centrality of *Euclid v. Ambler*," I found particularly useful the chapters by Arthur V. N. Brooks ("The Office File Box—Emanations from the Battlefield") and William M. Randle ("Professors, Reformers, Bureaucrats, and Cronies: The Players in *Euclid v. Ambler*"). Other valuable accounts of the case, its history and effects, include David Callies, "Village of Euclid

v. Ambler Realty Co.," in Gerald Korngold and Andrew P. Morriss, editors, *Property Stories* (New York: Foundation Press, 2004); Richard H. Chused, "*Euclid's* Historical Imagery," 51 *Case Western Reserve Law Review* 597 (2001); Garrett Power, "Advocates at Cross-Purposes: The Briefs on Behalf of Zoning in the Supreme Court," 2 *Journal of Supreme Court History 1997*, at 79; Michael Allan Wolf, "'Compelled by Conscientious Duty': *Village of Euclid v. Ambler Realty Co.* as Romance," 2 *Journal of Supreme Court History 1997*, at 88; Ruth Eckdish Knack, "Return to Euclid," *Planning*, November 1, 1996, at 4; Timothy Alan Fluck, "*Euclid v. Ambler*: A Retrospective," 52 *Journal of the American Planning Association* 326 (1986); and A. Dan Tarlock, "*Euclid* Revisited," *Land Use Law and Zoning Digest*, January 1982, at 4.

Following the lead of James Metzenbaum's early account in *The Law of Zoning* (New York: Baker, Voorhis and Company, 1930), several law school casebooks and treatises contain accounts of the case, its background, and its aftermath, including Stuart Meck and Kenneth Pearlman, *Ohio Planning and Zoning Law* (2007 edition, Eagan, Minn.: Thomson West); Daniel R. Mandelker, John Payne, Peter W. Salsich, Jr., and Nancy E. Stroud, *Planning and Control of Land Development: Cases and Materials* (6th edition, New York: Lexis Publishing, 2005); Robert C. Ellickson and Vicki L. Been, *Land Use Controls: Cases and Materials* (3d edition, Gaithersburg, Md.: Aspen Law and Business, 2005); Daniel R. Mandelker, *Land Use Law* (5th edition, Newark, N.J.: Matthew Bender, 2003); Charles M. Haar and Michael Allan Wolf, *Land-Use Planning: A Casebook on the Use, Misuse, and Re-use of Urban Land* (4th edition, Boston: Little, Brown and Company, 1989). For a fascinating account of Newton Baker's successful challenge to another Cleveland suburb's zoning ordinance as applied, see Stuart Meck, "Zoning and Anti-Semitism in the 1920s: The Case of *Cleveland Jewish Orphan Home v. Village of University Heights* and Its Aftermath," 4 *Journal of Planning History* 91 (2005).

Of the many histories of Cleveland, the reader will find most helpful Carol Poh Miller and Robert Anthony Wheeler, *Cleveland: A Concise History, 1796–1996* (Bloomington: Indiana University Press, 1997); and David D. Van Tassel and John J. Grabowski, editors, *Cleveland: A Tradition of Reform* (Kent, Ohio: Kent State University Press, 1986). The story of Bessie Benner Metzenbaum Park can be found in Jay Abercrombie, *Walks and Rambles in Ohio's Western Reserve: Discovering Nature and History in the Northeastern Corner* (Woodstock, Vt.: Backcountry Publications, 1996). I found details on the Van Sweringen brothers and the empire they built and lost in Herbert H. Harwood, Jr., *Invisible Giants: The Empires of Cleveland's Van Sweringen Brothers* (Bloomington: Indiana University Press, 2003); and Ian S. Haberman, *The Van Sweringens of Cleveland: The Biography of an Empire* (Cleveland, Ohio: Western Reserve Historical Society, 1979).

Full-volume biographies of the justice who wrote the majority opinion and of Ambler Realty's counsel are Hadley Arkes, *The Return of George Sutherland: Restoring a Jurisprudence of Natural Rights* (Princeton, N.J.: Princeton University Press, 1994); Joel Francis Paschal, *Mr. Justice Sutherland: A Man against the State* (Princeton, N.J.: Princeton University Press, 1951); and C. H. Cramer, *Newton Baker: A Biography* (Cleveland, Ohio: World Publishing Company, 1961). For additional biographical information on the members of the Taft Court, I turned to G. Edward White, *Justice Oliver Wendell Holmes: Law and the Inner Self* (New York: Oxford University Press, 1993); Alpheus Thomas Mason, *Harlan Fiske Stone: Pillar of the Law* (New York: Viking Press, 1956); Edward A. Purcell, Jr., *Brandeis and the Progressive Constitution: Erie, the Judicial Power, and the Politics of the Federal Courts in Twentieth-Century America* (New Haven, Conn.: Yale University Press, 2000); Robert C. Post, "The Supreme Court Opinion as Institutional Practice: Dissent, Legal Scholarship, and Decisionmaking in the Taft Court," 85 *Minnesota Law Review* 1267 (2001); Robert C. Post, "Defending the Lifeworld: Substantive Due Process in the Taft Court Era," 78 *Boston University Law Review* 1489 (1998); Barry Cushman, "The Secret Lives of the Four Horsemen," 83 *Virginia Law Review* 559 (1997); Alfred McCormack, "A Law Clerk's Recollections," 46 *Columbia Law Review* 710 (1946); and Melvin I. Urofsky, editor, *Biographical Encyclopedia of the Supreme Court: The Lives and Legal Philosophies of the Justices* (Washington, D.C.: CQ Press, 2006).

For the development of American suburbs and edge cities and for the New Urbanist fight against sprawl, see Dolores Hayden, *Building Suburbia: Green Fields and Urban Growth 1820–2000* (New York: Pantheon Books, 2003); Robert Fishman, *Bourgeois Utopias: The Rise and Fall of Suburbia* (New York: Basic Books, 1987); Andres Duany, Elizabeth Plater-Zyberk, and Jeff Speck, *Suburban Nation: The Rise of Sprawl and the Decline of the American Dream* (New York: North Point Press, 2000); Joel Garreau, *Edge City: Life on the New Frontier* (New York: Doubleday, 1991); John Stilgoe, *Borderland: Origins of the American Suburb, 1820–1939* (New Haven, Conn.: Yale University Press, 1988); Kenneth T. Jackson, *Crabgrass Frontier: The Suburbanization of the United States* (New York: Oxford University Press, 1985); Sam Bass Warner, Jr., *Streetcar Suburbs: The Process of Growth in Boston, 1870–1900* (2d edition, Cambridge. Mass.: Harvard University Press, 1978); and David Rusk, *Cities without Suburbs* (Washington, D.C.: Woodrow Wilson Center Press, 1993). On the development of subdivisions and the use of restrictive covenants and other private planning devices, see Robert M. Fogelson, *Bourgeois Nightmares: Suburbia, 1870-1930* (New Haven, Conn.: Yale University Press, 2005); Evan McKenzie, *Privatopia: Homeowner Associations and the Rise of Residential Private Government* (New Haven, Conn: Yale University Press, 1994); Marc A. Weiss, *The Rise of the Community Builders: The American Real*

Estate Industry and Urban Land Planning (New York: Columbia University Press, 1987); Gerald Korngold, "The Emergence of Private Land Use Controls in Large-Scale Subdivisions: The Companion Story to Village of *Euclid v. Ambler Realty Co.*," 51 *Case Western Reserve Law Review* 617 (2001); and Timothy Stoltzfus Jost, "The Defeasible Fee and the Birth of the Modern Residential Subdivision," 49 *Missouri Law Review* 695 (1984). For historical treatments of prezoning methods of land-use regulation, see John F. Hart, "Land Use Law in the Early Republic and the Original Meaning of the Takings Clause," 94 *Northwestern University Law Review* 1099 (2000); Joseph Gordon Hylton, "Prelude to *Euclid*: The United States Supreme Court and the Constitutionality of Land Use Regulation, 1900–1920," 3 *Washington University Journal of Law and Policy* 1 (2000); Mark Fenster, " 'A Remedy on Paper': The Role of Law in the Failure of City Planning in New Haven, 1907–1913," 107 *Yale Law Journal* 1093 (1998); and John F. Hart, "Colonial Land Use and Its Significance for Modern Takings Doctrine," 109 *Harvard Law Review* 1252 (1996). An interesting study of one important American city's experience is *Boston's "Changeful Times": Origins of Preservation and Planning in America* (Baltimore, Md.: Johns Hopkins University Press, 1998).

For further reading on the national movement that inspired modern American land-use planning laws and practices, see William H. Wilson, *The City Beautiful Movement* (Baltimore, Md.: Johns Hopkins University Press, 1989). For a riveting and best-selling book that includes details on the 1893 World's Columbian Exposition, see Erik Larson, *The Devil in the White City: Murder, Magic, and Madness at the Fair That Changed America* (New York: Crown Publishers, 2003). An essential source for understanding the ideas and personalities behind the American movement for land-use planning and zoning laws are the Proceedings of the National Conferences on City Planning, many of which are available online at http://www.archive.org/index .php. Other important primary sources include Alfred Bettman, *City and Regional Planning Papers* (Cambridge, Mass.: Harvard University Press, 1946); Advisory Committee on Planning and Zoning of the U.S. Department of Commerce, *A Standard City Planning Enabling Act* (Washington, D.C.: Government Printing Office, 1928), Department of Commerce, Advisory Committee on Zoning, *A Standard State Zoning Enabling Act: Under Which Municipalities May Adopt Zoning Regulations* (Washington, D.C.: Government Printing Office, 1926) (the latter two are available on the American Planning Association's website: https://www.planning.org/growingsmart/enabling acts.htm). See also Ruth Knack, Stuart Meck, and Israel Stollman, "The Real Story behind the Standard Planning and Zoning Acts of the 1920s," *Land Use Law & Zoning Digest*, February, 1996, at 3. Alfred Bettman's contributions to the victory in *Euclid v. Ambler* are celebrated in Robert Averill Walker, *The Planning Function in Urban Government* (Chicago: University of Chicago

Press, 1941). In *"Euclid* Lives: The Survival of Progressive Jurisprudence," 115 *Harvard Law Review* 2158 (2002), Charles Haar and I argue that Justice Sutherland's opinion in *Euclid v. Ambler* should continue to serve as a lodestar for the Supreme Court in analyzing a wide range of public regulation. For two recent, more critical appraisals of the motivations of early zoning proponents, see Eric A. Claeys, *"Euclid* Lives? The Uneasy Legacy of Progressivism in Zoning," 73 *Fordham Law Review* 731 (2004); and Martha A. Lees, "Preserving Property Values? Preserving Proper Homes? Preserving Privilege?: The Pre-*Euclid* Debate over Zoning for Exclusively Private Residential Areas, 1916–1926," 56 *University of Pittsburgh Law Review* 367 (1994).

Readers interested in exploring further the ideas of American Progressivism that engendered judicial and popular support for zoning should consult Richard Hofstadter's masterful treatment, *The Age of Reform: From Bryan to F.D.R.* (New York: Knopf, 1955); Barbara Miller Solomon's important study, *Ancestors and Immigrants: A Changing New England Tradition* (Cambridge, Mass.: Harvard University Press, 1956); and Frederic C. Howe's classic work, *The City: The Hope of Democracy* (New York: Charles Scribner's Sons, 1905). A provocative recent comparative study of Progressivism is Daniel T. Rodgers, *Atlantic Crossings: Social Politics in a Progressive Age* (Cambridge, Mass.: Harvard University Press, 1998). See also Michael McGerr, *A Fierce Discontent: The Rise and Fall of the Progressive Movement in America, 1870–1920* (New York: Free Press, 2003). On the rise of professionalism in America, see Burton J. Bledstein, *The Culture of Professionalism: The Middle Class and the Development of Higher Education in America* (New York: Norton, 1976).

Legal commentary on the validity and wisdom of zoning predates *Euclid v. Ambler* and continues to this day. Early examples include articles by two of the attorneys who defended the concept in their arguments to the Supreme Court: James Metzenbaum, "The History of Zoning—'A Thumbnail Sketch,'" 9 *Western Reserve Law Review* 36 (1957); Alfred Bettman, "The Decision of the Supreme Court of the United States in the Euclid Village Zoning Case," 1 *University of Cincinnati Law Review* 188 (1927); Alfred Bettman, "The Constitutionality of Zoning," 37 *Harvard Law Review* 837 (1924); and Alfred Bettman, "City Planning Progress: Cincinnati," 6 *National Municipal Review* 351 (1917). By the end of the twentieth century, the chorus of voices in opposition to zoning as practiced by local governments grew louder. Three influential works questioning the efficiency and constitutionality of zoning and other government land-use restrictions are Richard A. Epstein, *Takings: Private Property and the Power of Eminent Domain* (Cambridge. Mass.: Harvard University Press, 1985); Bernard H. Siegan, *Land Use without Zoning* (Lexington, Mass: Lexington Books, 1972); and Robert C. Ellickson, "Alternatives to Zoning: Covenants, Nuisance Rules, and Fines as Land Use Controls," 40 *University of Chicago Law Review* 681 (1973). Even staunch defenders of government regulation have recognized the potential for abuse. For example, the story of the fight against exclusionary zoning in New Jersey is told skillfully by Charles M. Haar in *Suburbs under Siege: Race, Space, and Audacious Judges* (Princeton, N.J.: Princeton University Press, 1996). My own contribution to the cautionary literature is Michael Allan Wolf, "*Euclid* at Threescore Years and Ten: Is This the Twilight of Environmental and Land-use Regulation?," 30 *University of Richmond Law Review* 961 (1996).

INDEX